IN THE PICTURE

IN THE PICTURE:

Production Stills from the TCM Archives

Introduction by Robert Osborne

Text by Alexa L. Foreman, Ruth A. Peltason, Mark A. Vieira

CHRONICLE BOOKS

SAN FRANCISCO

Library of Congress Cataloging-in-Publication Data available.

ISBN 0-8118-4416-1

Manufactured in Hong Kong.

Design by Vanessa Dina.

Distributed in Canada by Raincoast Books
9050 Shaughnessy Street
Vancouver, British Columbia V6P 6E5

10 9 8 7 6 5 4 3 2 1

Chronicle Books LLC
85 Second Street
San Francisco, California 94105
www.chroniclebooks.com

SPECIAL THANKS

To Roger Mayer, president, Turner Entertainment Co., a trailblazer in film preservation and restoration and a driving force in the movement to save our film heritage.

ACKNOWLEDGMENTS

In appreciation of all the individuals and organizations who helped find the treasures featured in this book and share our dedication to film preservation: from the Academy of Motion Picture Arts and Sciences & Margaret Herrick Library, Sue Guldin and Faye Thompson; from the George Eastman House, Anthony L'Abbate, Douglas Bicket, and Joseph Cameron; from the Warner Bros. Corporate Image Archive, Cynthia Graham and Steven Bingen; from the Wisconsin Center for Film and Theater Research, Dorinda Hartmann; and freelance film researcher, Woolsey Ackerman.

TCM contributors to project development and management, editorial and research, include Carrie Beers, Katherine Evans, Alexa Foreman, Tom Karsch, Heather Margolis, Robert Osborne, and Eric Weber.

Thanks to our friends and colleagues for their relentless enthusiasm and commitment to TCM: Brooks Branch, Creative Branding Group; Ruth Peltason, Bespoke Books; Mark Vieira, The Starlight Studio.

"HOLD FOR STILLS!"

That's a phrase that used to be shouted on motion picture sets as often as "Roll 'em!" "Cut!" "It's a print!" and "Let's try another!" (Or, if it was a Garbo set, "No visitors!") What those first three little words meant was that it was time for the still photographer to have his moment. As soon as the cinematographer captured a scene on film—be it Rhett Butler telling Scarlett O. he didn't give a damn, Julie Adams getting her first look at the Creature from the Black Lagoon, or Lana Turner giving John Garfield a smooch—the still photographer would emerge from the shadows to begin snapping still photographs of the same scene. He would place his camera in the very spot the movie camera had just been, and the actors would re-create the moment they had just acted—this time, however, posed and "frozen." Once the deed was done and the still photographer satisfied, everyone would then prep for the next sequence to be filmed.

So it went, day in, day out, and on every movie set in Hollywood. Many considered taking still photographs an irritant in a busy workday but, during an era when access to studio soundstages was extremely limited and the public's only entrance to a film set was through a movie studio's publicity department, it was also deemed a necessity. And thanks to those blessed still photographers, we have images of films and actors preserved in a unique way that, amazingly, has had little public exposure—until now.

Numerous tomes have been published that show the marvelous work done by Hollywood portrait artists such as George Hurrell, John Engsted, Clarence Sinclair Bull, and their peers with awesome images of Garbo, Dietrich, Gable, Crawford, Cooper, and others, posed in doorways, on ladders and leopard skins, in evening clothes or outlandish costumes. But to my knowledge, there's never been a book devoted to the work of those many talented (and usually unidentified) still photographers who were on a set day after day, recording Hollywood at work. That book is finally here.

There were several reasons why these on-the-set still photographers became such an essential part of the moviemaking system of their time. For one thing, their photographs were kept in a Set Reference book on each film, documenting all the various costumes and hairstyles worn, as well as the sets used and the way those sets were lit and dressed—which props were on which table, what painting was hanging where. With photographic evidence, any costume could be righted, any hairstyle corrected, any set reproduced exactly should the need arise.

The still photographer was also on the set, morning until quitting time, to record for posterity special occasions such as actors' birthdays (as when Olivia de Havilland celebrated her twenty-third birthday during the filming of *Gone with the Wind*) or special set visits (as when the rascally George Bernard Shaw made a famous visit to MGM in the 1930s and Judy Garland dropped by to chat with Ginger Rogers on the set of *The Barkleys of Broadway*, a film Judy was supposed to have done).

Most often, however, those photos (the best ones, of course) were considered essential publicity tools, zealously controlled by a studio's publicity department, some picked for poster art, others dispensed to magazine and newspaper editors to publicize the films and, at the same time, help satisfy the public's craving for any images or information available on their favorite stars. Photographs that are so familiar to us today—Gene Kelly hanging on the lamppost while he's "singin' in the rain," Clark Gable and Vivien Leigh in a passionate embrace in *Gone with the Wind*, Errol Flynn on a staircase, sword in hand, dueling with Basil Rathbone in *The Adventures of Robin Hood*, or Orson Welles as Charles Foster Kane standing at the podium—are all the work of a still photographer. All were posed. They just look as if they were a moment captured from the film itself.

Behind-the-scenes stills were also a prerogative of the studios, again for use in the publicity machine—a teenage Elizabeth Taylor studying her schoolbooks while waiting for a set to be workable, Carole Lombard playing poker with the crew, Fred and Ginger rehearsing their "Cheek to Cheek" number. So—why did the still photographer ultimately disappear from film sets? One reason is that budget cuts became a part of the Hollywood landscape in the 1950s as movie attendance dwindled with the initial impact of television. Still photographers, like contract players and full-time crew members, were among the first to go; soon after, costumers like Edith Head and Charles LeMaire, instead of specifically designing clothes for stars as in years past, began buying off the rack at local department stores. The "company" days were over and soon independent photographers began being assigned to cover movies on a day-by-day basis. After that, the death of upscale movie magazines and the birth of the paparazzi further changed the landscape forever.

That's one reason I found this book so entertaining to wander through. There's Rick saying good-bye to Ilsa at the airport in *Casablanca* as a camera and cameramen peer at them, reminding me that Humphrey Bogart and Ingrid Bergman were far from alone while making their "We'll always have Paris" farewell. There's also photographic proof that one of the most intimate moments in *Camille* between Greta Garbo and Robert Taylor was anything but as director George Cukor and a mini-army of crew members watch the lovers vow their undying passion. Look how many people it took to help Judy Garland and Mickey Rooney show they "got rhythm" in *Girl Crazy*. You'll be seeing familiar images from films you'll never forget as well as some less recognizable faces from movies you may not have seen, but the photos are endlessly fascinating. They remind us better than written words ever could that moviemaking is, indeed, a business and a collaborative effort.

The stills on these pages also reveal the true extent of Hollywood's sleight of hand: how entire villages, such as Munchkinland, were built inside soundstages, how airplanes—so realistic when seen in movies like *Thirty Seconds Over Tokyo*—were actually prop models and incomplete, as were those huge ships that look so seaworthy in *Captain Blood* and *Hearts Divided*. Houses complete with swimming pools as in *High Society* are, we see thanks to a still photographer, nothing more than a temporary workplace for actors. Does it spoil the magic? Not a whit. For me, these fascinating photographs only increase my admiration and respect for those people who have added so much entertainment, and so many dreams, to our lives through their work. And work it was. The amazing thing is how easy those artists have made it look. I hope you enjoy the journey behind the scenes. I certainly did. And Turner Classic Movies is delighted to be able to share the adventure with you.

—**ROBERT OSBORNE,** *host of Turner Classic Movies*

Unit still photographers at the newly merged Metro-Goldwyn-Mayer studios in 1924 faced a tough assignment. Using bulky 8x10 view cameras, they had to capture the excitement, the scope, and the glamour of the largest film production yet mounted in Hollywood—*Ben-Hur: A Tale of the Christ.* Its source was General Lew Wallace's 1897 novel, a blockbuster that sold second only to the Bible. *Ben-Hur* told the story of a rich Jewish youth who loses his position to slavery and his family to leprosy before Christ converts him. Citing the success of epics such as D. W. Griffith's *The Birth of a Nation,* Wallace's estate dared to ask an unheard-of $1 million for screen rights to *Ben-Hur.* No film company in the world could afford such a price, but when the Goldwyn Company offered a 50-percent split, a deal was made. As *Ben-Hur* began filming in Italy, the studio (whose namesake, Samuel Goldwyn, had long since left) began to rue the expensive production.

The first few months of shooting were hampered by problems usually encountered on location. Screenwriter June Mathis, who had earlier discovered Rudolph Valentino, could not find the right tone for her script, perhaps because she was not inspired by leading man George Walsh. Thousands of Italian extras idled on the beach while director Charles Brabin waited for alternate scenes to be written. When the new scenes were ready, the Italians went on strike. To all appearances, the Goldwyn Company was dumping the last of its cash into the Mediterranean.

In April 1924, Goldwyn joined the Metro and Mayer companies to create a bold new studio headquartered in the Culver City plant that had belonged to film pioneer Thomas Ince. The first order of business for MGM president Louis B. Mayer was to rein in the runaway *Ben-Hur.* In short order he replaced Mathis, Brabin, and Walsh. When a sinking galley nearly killed several Italian extras, he heeded the advice of production head Irving Thalberg and called the entire company back to California, where Fred Niblo directed Ramon Novarro as Judah Ben-Hur in picturesque scenes that looked as if they had been shot in the Holy Land. A showstopping chariot race was staged by second-unit director Reeves "Breezy" Eason with forty-two cameras and nearly four thousand extras. Behind-the-scenes stills of Novarro astride his chariot made by camera artist Ferdinand Pinney Earle whetted the public's appetite for this long-awaited epic. The photo on the opposite page shows Niblo and cameraman Percy Hilburn filming a scene of Carmel Myers as the Egyptian siren Iras.

After two years of shooting and reshooting, *Ben-Hur* was completed in late 1925. Its budget had reached a frightening $4 million. Griffith's *Intolerance* had not cost even half that, but it had sunk his company. Would *Ben-Hur* do the same to the fledgling MGM? Its December 1925 premiere told all. A superb blend of storytelling, showmanship, and sincerity, *Ben-Hur* eventually grossed more than $9 million (roughly $200 million in today's dollars) and set MGM on its way to becoming Hollywood's leading studio.

FLESH AND THE DEVIL | 19**26** | MGM

John Gilbert was twenty-nine and Greta Garbo was twenty-one when they met on this silent-
movie production. The screen chemistry was real; they fell in love and were teamed three additional
times (*Love*, *A Woman of Affairs*, and *Queen Christina*). According to director Clarence Brown
(shown at top), Gilbert was the more smitten of the two. "He was always proposing in front of
people . . . but she always kept him at arm's length."

THE SCARLET LETTER | 19**26** | MGM

Director Victor Seastrom gives legendary silent star Lillian Gish direction on set. Because of her
unusual contract with MGM, Gish chose her films and had approval of the director, cast, script, even
the time allotted for rehearsal. At age thirty-two, the waiflike talent was a fourteen-year veteran of
the screen and had amassed a considerable body of work with director D. W. Griffith.

12

THE CAMERAMAN 19**28** MGM

Buster Keaton and Edward Brophy rehearse the changing-room sequence in this silent film while
director Edward Sedgwick (seated) supervises. This was Keaton's favorite scene in the movie—in part
because it gave him latitude for a good deal of improvisation and because he and Brophy, men of different height and weight, switch clothes. It was also Keaton's first picture at MGM. Silent film relied
on gesture, and a clown as great as Keaton was a virtuoso of physical comedy. MGM was so pleased
with the result that the movie was shown as an example of how an MGM comedy should be made.

THE CAMERAMAN 1928 MGM

Director Edward Sedgwick consults with Buster Keaton on location in New York City.
Keaton had hoped to make the movie entirely in the city, but he had to settle for shooting only
a few scenes there because he drew so many crowds wherever he went.

THE MYSTERIOUS LADY | 19**28** | MGM

Musicians off camera set the mood for Greta Garbo and Conrad Nagel in this romantic picture
by silent-film director Fred Niblo. Cinematographer William Daniels is behind the camera.
Niblo, also the director of the mega-epic *Ben-Hur,* was an outspoken opponent of the talkies.

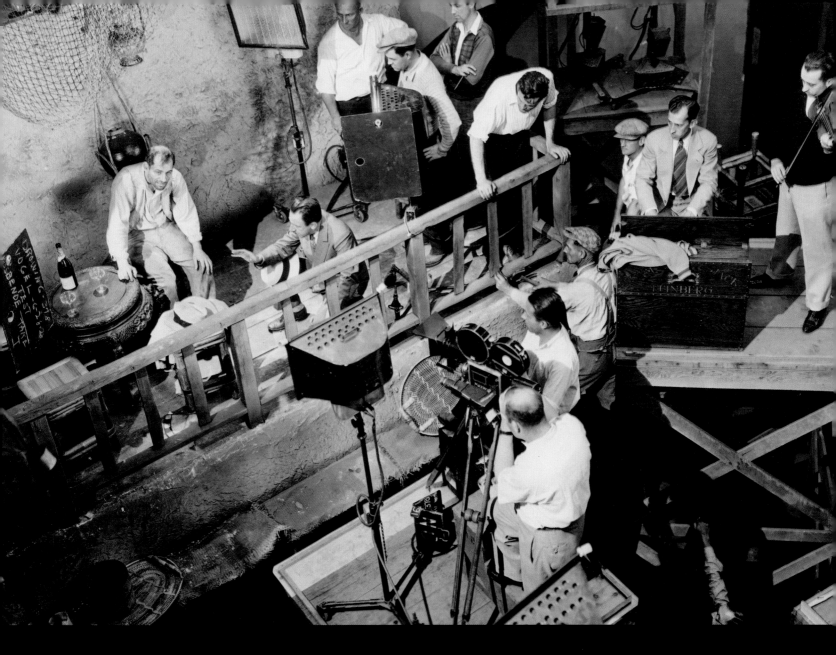

WEST OF ZANZIBAR | 19**28** | MGM

Lon Chaney, MGM's "man of a thousand faces," perfects a scowl for director Tod Browning, sitting. Chaney, who came to MGM with such films as *The Hunchback of Notre Dame* and *The Phantom of the Opera* already to his credit, originated the art of character acting in Hollywood and reigned as the world's number one box office attraction of his time. With Chaney on set are his personal musicians—Sam Feinberg on the organ and his brother Jack playing violin.

WHITE SHADOWS IN THE SOUTH SEAS | 19**28** | MGM

W. S. "Woody" Van Dyke directed MGM's first sound film with synchronized music
and sound effects, shot on location in Tahiti. The film opened in New York at the end of July
to record profits. In this image, Van Dyke directs actor Monte Blue.

THE HOLLYWOOD REVUE OF 1929 | 19**29** | MGM

Director Charles Reisner rehearses the film's final musical sequence, "Singin' in the Rain," on
an MGM soundstage with a cast that includes Polly Moran, Jack Benny, Marie Dressler, Buster
Keaton, Bessie Love, Cliff Edwards, and a young Joan Crawford. The studio was easing its silent
stars into the talking era with this all-star revue. The film is also interesting for the color segments,
such as the scene depicted here. As documented by a studio still photographer, this overhead
shot was used to capture the size and height of the set.

How do you take a picture of a voice? This was the challenge facing unit still photographer Milton Browne, whose behind-the-scenes photos of MGM's *Anna Christie* had to convey the excitement surrounding Greta Garbo's first sound film. A number of stars had already made disappointing "talkie" debuts. Audiences shook their heads at Norma Talmadge's Brooklyn accent, Corinne Griffith's lisp, and Vilma Banky's Hungarian accent. Most surprising was the reaction to John Gilbert's first talkie, *His Glorious Night*, released in September 1929 while Garbo was filming *Anna Christie*. When Gilbert said "I love you," fans who had swooned over his charismatic close-ups in *Flesh and the Devil* couldn't believe their ears. His voice was not high pitched, but a light baritone that did not match five years of fantasy. Shocked silence turned to nervous laughter. *His Glorious Night* flopped and fan magazines declared Gilbert a has-been.

Garbo had as much at stake. Her portrayals of free spirits in films like *The Mysterious Lady*, *The Divine Woman*, and *A Woman of Affairs* and her offscreen persona—private, unpretentious, single minded—had elevated her to a status unattained even by stars like Gloria Swanson and Mary Pickford. Playing no small part in this mesmerism were director Clarence Brown and cameraman William Daniels, who subordinated every cinematic element to Garbo's shimmering presence. For an international legion of fans, watching her glowing face projected forty feet tall on the screen of the local movie palace was a religious experience. What would happen when she spoke from that screen? Would the spell be broken? Would she be laughed at?

Garbo's talkie debut took place in Eugene O'Neill's Pulitzer Prize–winning *Anna Christie*, a play about a Swedish-American prostitute. Shooting in sequence, director Brown began with Anna's anxious entrance to the working-class tavern where her estranged father is getting drunk. On the first day of shooting, Garbo was as nervous as the character she was portraying. "I feel like an unborn child," she said on her way to the soundstage.

Photographer Browne first shot her sitting at a tavern table with director Brown, looking up at the microphone as if it were the Sword of Damocles. Garbo was used to posing for behind-the-scenes stills, but this was trying, since she was about to film an entire scene in one take—and with dialogue. Once she did and heard the sound disk played back, her mood lightened: "My God! Is that my voice?" The sound recordist pronounced the transcription a success, and Garbo relaxed enough for Browne to shoot carefully posed production stills. They appeared in every fan magazine in the world, and after *Anna Christie* became the highest-grossing film of 1930, MGM satisfied her European fans by having her make a German-language version of the film. Behind-the-scenes photos of her studying German with Daniels (who had helped her learn English on the set five years earlier) helped make the second *Anna Christie* a worldwide hit and established Garbo as the newest star of the talkies.

GOOD NEWS | 19**30** | MGM

Actor Delmer Daves waits as crew members adjust the camera while Bessie Love holds her position
under the bed. Although Daves acted in some late silent films and early talkies, he is best remembered
as a screenwriter and as the director of *Dark Passage. Good News* was remade in 1947, this time under
the watch of the prolific MGM musicals producer, Arthur Freed.

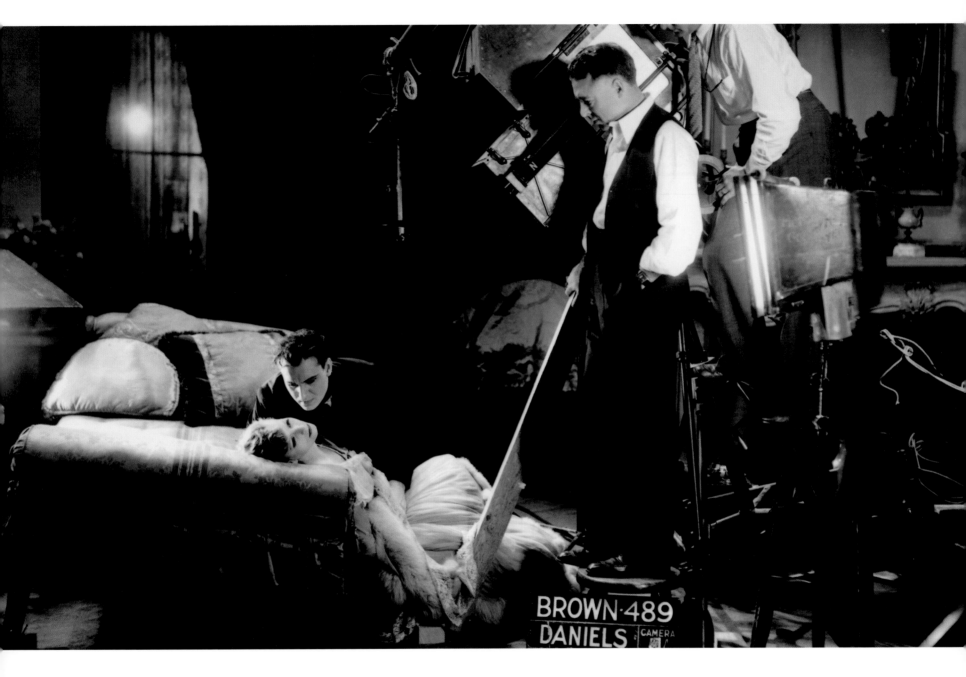

ROMANCE | 19**30** | MGM

Greta Garbo's second talking picture teamed her with Gavin Gordon, although her choice had been Gary Cooper. Both Garbo and director Clarence Brown were nominated for Academy Awards. Cinematographer William Daniels stands above Brown. Owing to the increased weight of the new camera blimp, which was designed by MGM camera department head John Arnold, even a slightly elevated shot could not be made without a specially constructed wooden lift.

22

LITTLE CAESAR | 19**31** | WARNER BROS.

"Mother of Mercy! Is this the end of Rico?" With his short body, doughy nose, and inimitably nasal voice, Edward G. Robinson wouldn't seem the type to vault to stardom, but as Rico in *Little Caesar* the actor made his mark. Robinson, who was forever associated with this performance, was a reliable stalwart for Warner Bros., where he worked for more than a decade. In this image he's seen with Maurice Black, George E. Stone, and Noel Madison. Director Mervyn LeRoy, who began the gangster cycle with this film, leans against the "Stage 17" platform at right.

LITTLE CAESAR | 19**31** | WARNER BROS.

Technicians set up a shot of a roulette wheel to be used as part of a montage sequence leading into a scene in the casino. Not only was *Little Caesar* a hit, it paved the way for the gangster films that flourished during the 1930s. Mervyn LeRoy, with a megaphone, is leaning over the camera platform, which was built because Warner Bros. did not yet have one of the newly invented camera cranes.

INSPIRATION | 19**31** | MGM

Filled with love triangles and love tangles, *Inspiration* stars Greta Garbo as the model Yvonne,
who is said to be "as well-known as the Eiffel Tower" and who falls for the handsome and
unpretentious student André (Robert Montgomery). Things go terribly wrong from here all the
way to the end. In this take, director Clarence Brown (in sweater) watches as Garbo and Montgomery
descend the stairs. Cinematographer William Daniels (in glasses) is behind the camera.
Note the still-unperfected microphone boom.

SUSAN LENOX: HER FALL AND RISE | 19**31** | MGM

Born out of wedlock, then pledged to a farmer who tries to ruin her just before their wedding, Susan Lenox
(Greta Garbo) seeks refuge at the home of Rodney Spencer (Clark Gable), who happens to be a dashing and darling
young engineer. Love blossoms, love is thwarted, and in the end, the true lovers reunite. This photo was taken early
in the film's production and includes director Robert Z. Leonard and cinematographer William Daniels. The scene,
which was ultimately cut, was filmed near the Franklin Union Reservoir in the Hollywood Hills.

Unit still photographer Milton Browne was used to making a star look good, both in scene stills and behind-the-scenes stills. This is why he was Greta Garbo's favorite on-the-set "stills man." Occasionally he had to make two stars look good, as in the case of *Mata Hari*, in which Garbo costarred with Ramon Novarro. In January 1932, on an MGM soundstage that had been transformed into an art deco hotel, he had the formidable assignment of shooting five stars in one film. Edmund Goulding's *Grand Hotel* was going into production and it boasted Hollywood's first all-star cast: Wallace Beery, John Barrymore, Joan Crawford, Lionel Barrymore, and Garbo. How would Browne make each famous face look good without making the other faces in the photo feel that they were getting second best? After all, rehearsals had begun with Beery stomping out, saying that he would come back when Crawford learned how to act. And the Barrymore brothers had exchanged words a few months before on the set of *Arsene Lupin*, accusing each other of upstaging. And Garbo had refused to pose with visitors to the set since having to stand next to a maharajah on *Anna Christie*.

As it turned out, the stars were so intimidated by Irving Thalberg's casting coup that they behaved admirably. Crawford recalled: "Every single day Mr. Lionel Barrymore would say something nice to me."

John Barrymore introduced himself to Garbo by saying: "My wife and I think you are the most beautiful woman in the world." Garbo returned the compliment after a few days of work with the Great Profile. She kissed him and said, "You have no idea what it means to me to play opposite so perfect an artist." Toward the end of filming, Garbo said to Crawford, "I'm so sorry we are not working together. What a pity, eh? Our first picture together and not one scene." John Barrymore, with a raised eyebrow, tolerated Beery's well-known rudeness and then worked with him in the scene in which Beery attacks him. Barrymore then said to Beery, "Not that I'm falling in love with you or anything, but I'd like to make a statement. You're the best actor on this set."

Vicki Baum, author of the novel *Grand Hotel*, came to that set when Garbo was working and was promptly asked to leave; Miss Garbo did not allow visitors while she was working. Garbo did, however, allow Browne to take photos of her sitting next to John Barrymore at the perimeter of the set. Baum accepted Garbo's behavior graciously. And why not? Garbo and her stellar colleagues made *Grand Hotel* a multimillion-dollar hit, even in the worst days of the Great Depression. And Milton Browne's distinguished photos did their utmost to sell it.

Following spread: *Grand Hotel*

EMMA | 19**32** | MGM

Marie Dressler, one of MGM's most popular comedic actresses in the 1930s, was nominated
for an Academy Award for this movie. With her is Richard Cromwell (in flight jacket),
whom the actress had asked MGM to cast in the part.

FREAKS | 19**32** | MGM

Tod Browning's bizarre and disturbing film of love and betrayal set in a traveling circus, cast
with real-life sideshow performers and human oddities, shocked and offended audiences of its day.
Banned in England, quickly buried by MGM (ironically, the studio that was recognized for its
sophistication and good taste), *Freaks* is widely considered a cult classic today.

FAITHLESS  19**32** MGM

Director Harry Beaumont watches Tallulah Bankhead and Robert Montgomery rehearse. The actress
was on loan from Paramount and returned to the stage following this rare screen appearance.
Beaumont, who turned to directing in 1915, is remembered as the director of the silents *Beau Brummell,*
starring John Barrymore, and *Our Dancing Daughters,* the film that launched Joan Crawford's career.

RED DUST | 19**32** | MGM

Jean Harlow and her platinum hair shine in this steamy romance with Clark Gable, the second of six films the pair made together. Off camera, Mary Astor and Gable take a break while Victor Fleming directs Harlow, who plays an on-the-lam floozie by the unlikely name of Vantine. Cinematographer Harold "Hal" Rosson is next to the camera. Fleming, who later became best known for directing *The Wizard of Oz* and taking over the reins of *Gone with the Wind*, began his career as a race-car driver and still photographer.

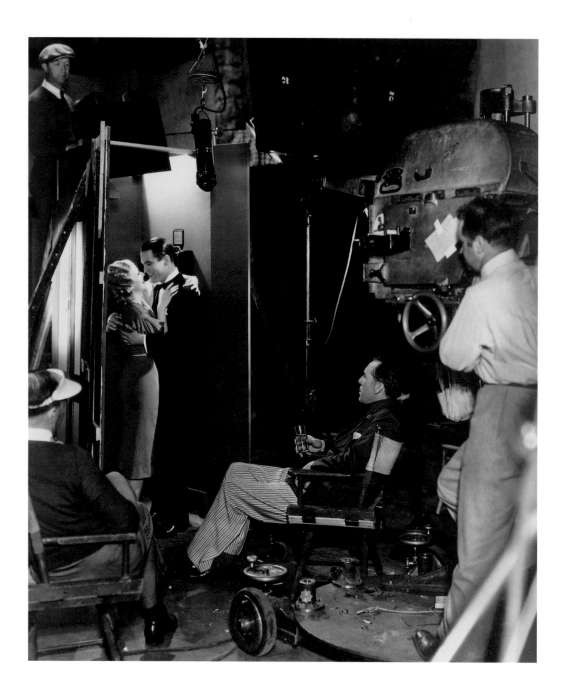

RED-HEADED WOMAN | 19**32** | MGM

Jack Conway (holding glass) directs Chester Morris and gold digger Jean Harlow.
The studio took a big risk by changing Harlow's hair color for the film, as it was
so much a part of her persona and allure.

STRANGE INTERLUDE | 19**32** | MGM

This compelling adaptation of Eugene O'Neill's play by the same name allows viewers to
hear what the characters think—often at variance with their on-screen behavior. The voice-overs
were achieved by playing back the actors' voices on an acetate disk as seen in this still.
Aside from the endless drama and entanglements in the story, the film is notable for giving audiences
a first look at Clark Gable with his trademark mustache in later scenes. The movie was the second
of three pictures Gable made with Norma Shearer.

TARZAN THE APE MAN | 19**32** | MGM

Director W. S. Van Dyke looks down on Maureen O'Sullivan and Johnny Weissmuller
for an overhead shot. This movie was the first sound version in MGM's series of six Tarzan
films starring former Olympic swim champion Weissmuller.

THE PRIZEFIGHTER AND THE LADY | 19**33** | MGM

Taking advantage of the popularity of champion boxers Primo Carnera, Jack Dempsey, and
Max Baer Sr., MGM cast them in this action romance costarring Myrna Loy, for whom W. S. Van Dyke
tailored the role. Here, Van Dyke directs Baer and Carnera in the ring. The following year, the two
duked it out for the heavyweight title, which Baer won.

FEMALE | 19**33** | WARNER BROS.

For a moment this could be construed as a tender love scene, but in *Female* Ruth Chatterton calls the shots with all her suitors—and there are many in this steamy film. Chatterton's Alison Drake is a smooth operator, both of an automobile factory and the men who work there. Only inventor Jim Thorne, played by Chatterton's real-life spouse George Brent, resists her seductions. (Brent and Chatterton divorced a year later.) The film was directed by Michael Curtiz, seen in the foreground.

HOLD YOUR MAN | 19**33** | MGM

Clark Gable takes a break while Jean Harlow is relit by cinematographer Hal Rosson.
Director Sam Wood is seated. Shortly after the film was released, Harlow and Rosson eloped.

QUEEN CHRISTINA | 19**33** | MGM

Greta Garbo asked that John Gilbert, her former costar, be cast as her leading man in
this film about the seventeenth-century Swedish monarch. They were directed by the gifted
Rouben Mamoulian, who among other things insisted that Garbo change her policy of
not rehearsing. Although the star felt rehearsing made her performance stale, she agreed
and in fact turned out a stellar performance.

KING KONG | 19**33** | RKO

An ape with a heart—who would imagine when we first see the twenty-four-foot King Kong on Skull Island? But through the brilliance of codirectors Merian C. Cooper and Ernest Schoedsack, and with artful animation effects created by Willis H. O'Brien, Kong has force, personality, and love in spades. What audiences didn't realize is that Kong was never once assembled as a full-sized ape but was made to appear so through editing. The film, one of the biggest box-office hits of the 1930s, is perhaps best remembered for the penultimate scene atop New York's Empire State Building, with Kong, Fay Wray, and four navy biplanes.

42

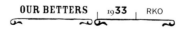

OUR BETTERS | 19**33** | RKO

Director George Cukor watches Minor Watson and Constance Bennett rehearse in this
film adapted from the play by W. Somerset Maugham. This was the third of five pictures in which
Cukor would direct Bennett. When she made this film, Bennett was considered a star, yet by the
1940s and 1950s when she was again directed by Cukor, she was best known as a character actress.
Not long after completing this movie, Cukor left RKO along with producer David O. Selznick
and went to MGM, where they collaborated on *Dinner at Eight.*

DINNER AT EIGHT | 19**33** | MGM

A near-flawless drawing-room comedy of social mores and manners, *Dinner at Eight* continues to entertain and instruct. Credit for the film goes to the play on which it was based by Edna Ferber and George Kaufman; script by Herman Mankiewicz, Frances Marion, and Donald Ogden Stewart (the clever repartee is priceless); direction by George Cukor; and an all-star cast, including Marie Dressler, Barrymores John and Lionel, Wallace Beery, and of course Jean Harlow, who in this image is flashing a smile at director Cukor.

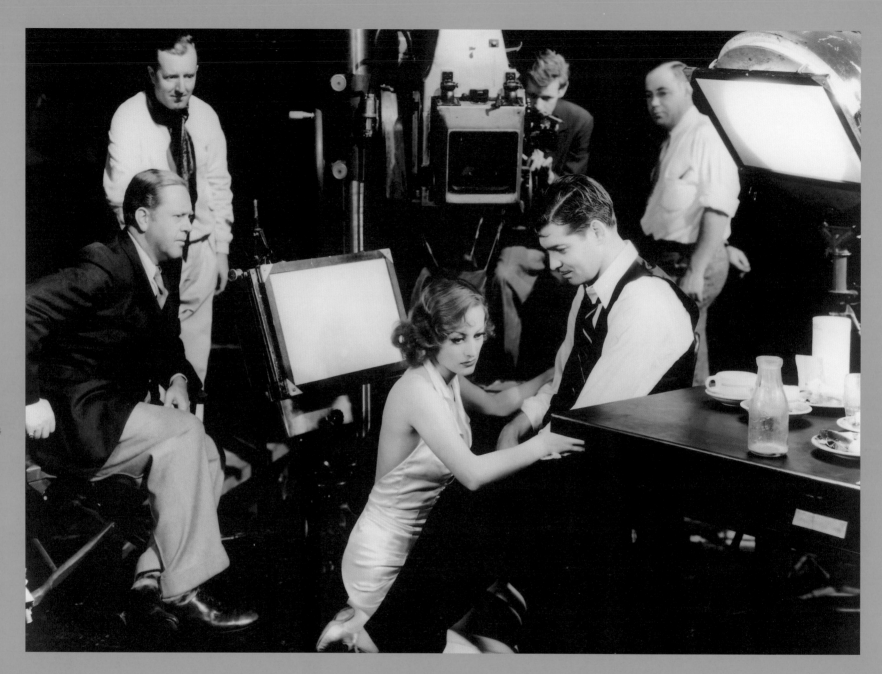

DANCING LADY | 19**33** | MGM

Joan Crawford plays a down-on-her-luck dancer and Clark Gable the director who initially does
what he can to thwart her career. The two stars, who had a long-running offscreen romance,
made eight films together. Here, they rehearse for director Robert Z. Leonard.

DANCING LADY | 19**33** | MGM

Dancing Lady hits the high mark as Joan Crawford and Fred Astaire (in his screen debut)
rehearse a dance sequence inside an MGM soundstage. The same year, Astaire was teamed up at
RKO with a young actress named Ginger Rogers for the film *Flying Down to Rio*.

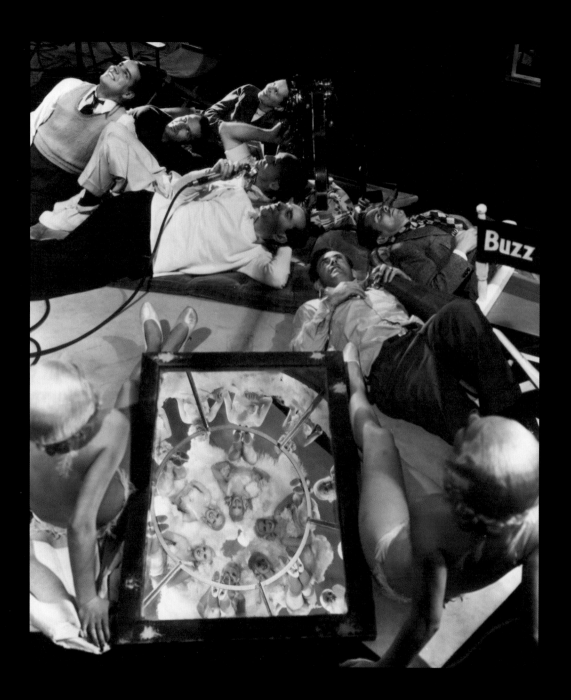

FASHIONS OF 1934 | 19**34** | WARNER BROS.

Choreographer Busby Berkeley, who made a name for himself directing musicals on Broadway,
was known for the kaleidoscopic patterns formed by his dancers as well as his famous "top shot"
technique, shown here and as reflected in the mirror (Berkeley is holding the microphone).
Incredibly, Berkeley used only one camera to catch the larger-than-life dance numbers in his movies.
The chair off to the right—stenciled "Buzz"—was of course Berkeley's.

WONDER BAR | 19**34** | WARNER BROS.

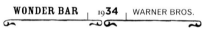

Busby Berkeley shows his dancers the emotion he wants conveyed in the film's "Don't Say Goodnight" sequence. The action reflected in the mirrors makes it appear that hundreds of dancers are used in this number. The movie was directed by Lloyd Bacon, part of the Warner Bros. stable of talent.

THE THIN MAN | 19**34** | MGM

MGM did not have high expectations for *The Thin Man*, which was made on a tight schedule and a low budget, but the film became a popular and critical winner and was ultimately followed by five sequels. Its success is largely credited to the brilliant repartee between Myrna Loy and William Powell (who made fourteen films together over the years). Here, William Powell rehearses a dinner scene with other members of the cast, including Maureen O'Sullivan (in hat) and Loy. The film, based on Dashiell Hammett's novel, received Academy Award nominations for Best Picture, Best Adapted Screenplay, Best Director (W. S. Van Dyke), and Best Actor (Powell).

50

MANHATTAN MELODRAMA | 19**34** | MGM

Clark Gable and William Powell play boyhood friends who face off as forces of good and evil in this crime drama. Powell plays good guy D.A. Jim Wade to Gable's gangster Blackie Gallagher. As for Myrna Loy, she's right in the middle as Blackie's former mistress now married to Wade, which adds considerable heat to the rivalry between the two men. The drama is enhanced by cinematographer James Wong Howe's lighting, which prefigures film noir by nearly a decade. Howe is to the left of Myrna Loy, on whose bed Powell and director W. S. Van Dyke are seated.

51

MANHATTAN MELODRAMA | 19**34** | MGM

James Wong Howe (standing) and W. S. Van Dyke (seated) watch Clark Gable spin the roulette wheel.
Nat Pendleton, with his hand on Gable's shoulder, plays Spud.

FORSAKING ALL OTHERS | 19**34** | MGM

Billie Burke and Clark Gable sit in a mock-up of a chauffeured car. Rear projection will be shown through the car window to give the illusion of a car in motion. This photograph is typical of the stills made by the studio's publicity department, for Burke and Gable are posing, not rehearsing or performing. Charles Butterworth joins them for the actual shot.

HIDE-OUT | 19**34** | MGM

W. S. Van Dyke sits in his director's chair while Robert Montgomery and Maureen O'Sullivan
hold a pose for a still photographer on the set. Because stills had to be sent to magazines as soon as
possible, the studios had publicity pictures taken early in production.

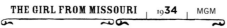

THE GIRL FROM MISSOURI | 19**34** | MGM

Jack Conway, seen here in Jean Harlow's dressing room, directed the star in four films, of which
The Girl from Missouri was the second. The last film was *Saratoga,* in 1937, which Harlow had nearly
completed before her sudden death. Here Harlow plays gold digger Eadie Chapman, who leaves her
Midwestern roots and travels to New York, determined to marry a man of means.

TARZAN AND HIS MATE | 19**34** | MGM

MGM's back lot doubled as the African jungle in the second—and most successful, according
to some critics—in the series of *Tarzan* films. Indications of pre-Code Hollywood are in
Maureen O'Sullivan's skimpy attire (not to mention the famous skinny-dipping scene) and the
fact that Jane and Tarzan have been happily cohabitating for two years, without either a marriage
license or church blessing. Subsequent *Tarzan* films were more family friendly.
Director Jack Conway is seen pointing to O'Sullivan.

Dance has been a part of the moviegoing experience since the days of the nickelodeons, when patrons put coins in a slot to watch flickering images of dancing girls dressed as gypsies. In the 1930s dance played a vital role in the fortunes of a struggling Hollywood studio. Founded in 1929 by financier Joseph P. Kennedy and Radio Corporation of America's David Sarnoff, RKO-Radio Pictures had neither the star power of MGM nor the theater chains of the Fox Film Corporation. The modest studio survived the first years of the Great Depression by making inexpensive comedies and occasional epics like *Cimarron* and *King Kong*, but by 1933 it was bankrupt. What RKO needed was a star who could consistently fill theater seats. By a happy accident, it got two.

Musicals were in vogue in 1933, but screen dancing was confined to the chorus girls of Warner Bros. spectaculars like *Gold Diggers of 1933*, in which a ubiquitous young actress named Ginger Rogers introduced the song "We're in the Money." Recognizing a good thing, RKO signed Rogers to a contract but did not cast her in its own supermusical, *Flying Down to Rio*, expecting that Dolores del Rio and dozens of shapely chorines would be enough to make a hit. In true show-business tradition, Rogers joined the cast when contract player Dorothy Jordan left suddenly to marry *King Kong* producer Merian C. Cooper. The renowned Broadway dancer Fred Astaire was getting attention for his debut in MGM's *Dancing Lady*, so RKO cast him opposite Rogers and gave them one dance number, "The Carioca." Rogers, who had her heart set on stardom as a dramatic actress, said to Astaire: "I don't want to do any more musicals, but I guess it'll turn out all right. Anyway, we'll have some fun."

Astaire and dance director Hermes Pan choreographed "The Carioca" in a manner new to the screen, as "an intimate dance number . . . which you see from start to finish." The number was expanded to include the obligatory chorus, but it was the graceful couple who got the notices and made the film a hit. Two other Rogers-Astaire pairings, *The Gay Divorcee* and *Roberta*, were also big successes in the mid-1930s. When *Top Hat* became the top-grossing film of 1935, it was obvious that Rogers and Astaire had saved RKO. *Top Hat's* still photographer used an 8x10 view camera to make these behind-the-scenes photos, so Rogers and Astaire had to assume poses representing their choreography. In the "Cheek to Cheek" number, Rogers wore a feathered gown that photographed beautifully in motion, but no still photo could be shot of the scene until a studio technician had removed stray feathers from the floor and from Astaire, who, according to Rogers, "muttered to himself as he plucked the feathers off his tailcoat." Not until the late 1930s, when both film and shutters became faster, was it possible to capture the spontaneous lyricism of their dancing—and the flying feathers.

Following spread: *Top Hat*

GOLD DIGGERS OF 1935 | 19**35** | WARNER BROS.

This was the second of the *Gold Diggers* films, and it shows off Busby Berkeley doing what he does best: lavish production numbers, precision choreography, and a guaranteed fantasy world at odds with the Depression taking place just outside the movie theaters. For this scene, Berkeley prepares a camera angle for the sequence "The Words Are in My Heart," which involved fifty-six pianos and girls, girls, girls!

CAPTAIN BLOOD | 19**35** | WARNER BROS.

Director Michael Curtiz, studio head Jack Warner, talent scout Solly Baiano, and Errol Flynn (in wig)
survey the ship set inside a Warner Bros. soundstage. The movie made a star of twenty-six-year-old
Flynn, who was cast at the last minute when actor Robert Donat had to drop out for health reasons.

A NIGHT AT THE OPERA | 19**35** | MGM

"The party of the first part shall hereafter be known as the party of the first part . . ." is only
a hint at the verbal and physical gags in what aficionados consider one of the best Marx Brothers
films. It was also their first film for MGM (they had previously been at Paramount), where they
were under the careful guidance of producer Irving Thalberg. Director Sam Wood watches as
Chico, Harpo, and Groucho Marx rehearse a scene.

A NIGHT AT THE OPERA | 19**35** | MGM

Sam Wood (standing) watches Groucho, Harpo, and Chico rehearse a routine with
Walter Woolf King, in costume. In all, the Marx Brothers made five movies for MGM.

RECKLESS | 19**35** | MGM

Jean Harlow and William Powell met in May 1934 when Powell signed with MGM.
The studio chose Powell for this film and subsequently replaced Joan Crawford with Harlow
when it became evident that Harlow and Powell were dating. To capitalize on the lovers' offscreen
romance, MGM cast Powell as Franchot Tone's rival in the film, who is seen here along
with Harlow and director Victor Fleming. The news about Powell and Harlow made great
headlines, all of which MGM was only too happy to supply.

NAUGHTY MARIETTA | 19**35** | MGM

This film was the first of the renowned Jeanette MacDonald and Nelson Eddy
collaborations and featured their famous duet, "Ah, Sweet Mystery of Life." As a period piece,
the film takes liberties with Victor Herbert's original libretto, all of which only sweetened the
film for audiences. Ed Keane (in wig) stands to the right of MacDonald.

SYLVIA SCARLETT | 19**35** | RKO

This was the first of four movies that Katharine Hepburn and Cary Grant made together.
Here, Grant (in still, left), and Natalie Paley and Hepburn (in still, right), pose for the camera
on location in Malibu. Director George Cukor later described the mood on this production
as ecstatic. Unfortunately, the critics did not feel the same way about the finished product,
although the film has gone on to become a cult classic.

HEARTS DIVIDED | 19**36** | WARNER BROS.

Dick Powell and Marion Davies pose as lovebirds Jérôme Bonaparte (brother of Napoleon) and
Betsy Patterson, a Baltimore beauty, for a still photographer as director Frank Borzage (in suit)
and cinematographer George Folsey watch. *Hearts Divided* was based on a true story, though the
ending was changed for more dramatic flair. Both ship and ocean are in a studio soundstage.

ROMEO AND JULIET | 19**36** | MGM

There were no fewer than a dozen film versions made in the twentieth century of Shakespeare's
famous play. At the top of the stack is the one produced by Irving Thalberg and directed by George
Cukor. So effective was the film that it didn't seem to matter that Thalberg's wife, Norma Shearer,
was too old to play Juliet (she was thirty-six) as was Leslie Howard (at forty-three) to play Romeo.
In this shot, Shearer rehearses with Ralph Forbes, with Cukor just off to the side.

SAN FRANCISCO | 19**36** | MGM

It's a contest of good versus evil, personified by Spencer Tracy as Father Tim Mullin and
Clark Gable as city-smart rake Blackie Norton, Father Mullin's former best friend turned foe.
In this scene, Father Tim is about to knock down Blackie in a friendly round of boxing at the gym.
The film, set around the San Francisco earthquake of 1906, was a hit for MGM.
Off to the side, director W. S. Van Dyke and actor Ted Healy watch.

70

LIBELED LADY | 19**36** | MGM

The cast for this lighthearted comedy included William Powell, Myrna Loy,
Jean Harlow, and Spencer Tracy. In the film's famous fishing scene, Powell gives fly-fishing a try.
The boom mike above Powell's head is recording sound.

THE PETRIFIED FOREST | 19**36** | WARNER BROS.

Director Archie Mayo (seated, in white shirt), the script girl, cinematographer Sol Polito
(under camera lens), and supporting cast and crew watch Humphrey Bogart, Bette Davis,
and Leslie Howard gather around a rock inside a Warner Bros. soundstage. The man seated
at the far right is actor Charley Grapewin, who is best known today as Uncle Henry in
The Wizard of Oz, a film he appeared in three years later.

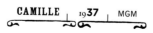

CAMILLE | 19**37** | MGM

Greta Garbo brings high glamour and radiance to this period film as Alexandre Dumas's doomed heroine.
Garbo's allure as a Parisian courtesan was enhanced by the great MGM costume designer Adrian, whom she
trusted implicitly. Adrian, who deemed that "costume was character," believed that the sign of a "kept woman"
lay in the extravagance of her dress. To this end, he had Garbo in luxurious, over-the-top confections. In this
scene, the sparkling stars on Garbo's off-the-shoulder dress suggest her character's dazzling beauty before Robert
Taylor, who plays her lover, Armand. On the set are George Cukor and William Daniels, behind the camera.

MAYTIME 19**37** MGM

This was the third of eight films teaming singing duo Jeanette MacDonald and Nelson Eddy;
it was also MacDonald's personal favorite. Here, Eddy mouths the words to "Will You Remember"
to a playback of his voice on an MGM soundstage.

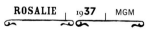
ROSALIE | 19**37** | MGM

The musical extravaganza *Rosalie* abounded in some great songs, among them "In the Still
of the Night" and "Spring Love Is in the Air." On lavish sets designed by Cedric Gibbons,
enormous dance numbers featured the great dancer Eleanor Powell, seen here in a flared
black-and-white skirt to the left of the camera.

SHALL WE DANCE | 19**37** | RKO

Shall We Dance was the seventh of the Astaire-Rogers films, five of which were directed
by Mark Sandrich, seen in the director's chair. The Gershwin score included the song
"They All Laughed," which Ginger Rogers is rehearsing.

THE PRINCE AND THE PAUPER | 1937 | WARNER BROS.

Bobby and Billy Mauch, identical twins who were radio personalities, were handpicked to
make the dramatic caper *The Prince and the Pauper*. Errol Flynn is given top billing, although
his role was actually less central to the story. Director William Keighley (in coat) and
cinematographer Sol Polito observe the action.

TOVARICH | 19**37** | WARNER BROS.

Claudette Colbert as the Grand Duchess Tatiana Petrovna, Charles Boyer as her husband,
Prince Mikail Alexandrovitch Ouratieff, and Basil Rathbone as Gorotchenko lead the way in this
lighthearted drama set in France. Director Anatole Litvak (seated with script) watches while Boyer
and Colbert rehearse a scene with Rathbone and Isabel Jeans, each seated close to Colbert.

NIGHT MUST FALL | 19**37** | MGM

Robert Montgomery and Rosalind Russell smile in a posed shot beside a wheelchair that
Montgomery is oiling. In the actual scene there are no smiles; instead Montgomery whistles a tune
that Russell realizes ties him to a murder. Director Richard Thorpe (with script) watches.
Montgomery's performance was nominated for an Academy Award.

BRINGING UP BABY | 19**38** | RKO

One of the quintessential screwball comedies of the 1930s. In this case, "Baby" is a pet leopard
belonging to an heiress (Katharine Hepburn). In her romantic pursuit of a nerdish paleontologist
(Cary Grant), both stars wind up in jail, a result of comedic error involving a dog, a dinosaur bone,
and the leopard. On the ladder behind Hepburn is director Howard Hawks.

JEZEBEL | 19**38** | WARNER BROS.

Henry Fonda and Bette Davis prepare to shoot the "red dress at the ball" scene. Though in fact brown,
Davis's dress looked red when shot in black-and-white. Director William Wyler stands behind Fonda along
with cinematographer Ernest Haller on Wyler's right. Fonda's daughter Jane had just been born, so the
star was permitted to finish his scenes early so he could be with his wife. After Fonda left, Wyler demanded
additional takes—he was notorious for doing so—leaving Davis to shoot her close-ups without a leading
man to play to. Nevertheless, she won the Academy Award for Best Actress.

ANDY HARDY GETS SPRING FEVER | 19**39** | MGM

W. S. Van Dyke (in light-colored suit) directs Mickey Rooney and Lewis Stone in a father-and-son chat, a regular component of MGM's popular *Andy Hardy* series. In this film, the seventh out of sixteen in the series, Andy develops a crush on his high-school drama teacher, something Judge Hardy knows is bound to backfire (which of course it does).

Nineteen thirty-nine was a watershed year if there ever was one. Politics, science, and art all felt the chill winds of change. Hollywood was no exception. The studio system was at the height of its power, the fourth largest industry in America, but a war could cut off its lucrative European market. In a burst of commerce and creativity, Hollywood produced a portfolio of motion pictures that would set a standard of excellence for decades to come. This portfolio included Columbia's *Mr. Smith Goes to Washington;* Universal's *Son of Frankenstein;* Goldwyn's *Wuthering Heights;* United Artists' *Stagecoach;* RKO's *The Hunchback of Notre Dame;* Warner Bros.' *Dark Victory;* Paramount's *Union Pacific;* Twentieth Century-Fox's *The Rains Came;* MGM's *The Wizard of Oz;* and, of course, David O. Selznick's *Gone with the Wind.*

In order to fix *Gone with the Wind* in the public's mind as a special event (and to recoup its $4.1 million cost), Selznick presented it in reserved-seat road-show engagements, charged higher ticket prices, and spent hundreds of thousands of dollars on publicity. Billboards and radio helped sell the film, but it was photography that made the public accept the new release formula; its "key set" of stills contained over 1000 tantalizing photographs.

Behind-the-scenes photography in 1939 looked distinctly different than it had five years earlier. New technology had brought faster films, lighter cameras, and shutters that could freeze action. The cumbersome 5x7 camera, which had to be held at waist level in order to capture an action shot, had been replaced by the 4x5 press camera, which could

be held up to the photographer's eye. Its smaller negatives, however, could not be printed by the 8x10 contact printing machine that made the thousands of 8x10 glossy photographs sent out by the studio, so the laboratory enlarged the 4x5 negatives to 8x10 duplicate negatives. The new, unposed look of behind-the-scenes stills was influenced by magazines like *Pic, Look,* and *Life,* who had popularized the terms "candid" and "grab shot" with photos that froze dramatic action as it happened, whether on the playing field or on the battlefield. Editors of *Photoplay* and dozens of other fan magazines now expected Hollywood to deliver the same kind of images. No more posed, painterly behind-the-scenes portraits. Spontaneity was the order of the day.

Photographers on *The Wizard of Oz* and *Gone with the Wind* also had to show a public familiar with the literary sources of these films how their beloved characters would transfer to the screen. How would Dorothy Gale and Scarlett O'Hara look? The Land of Oz and antebellum Atlanta? Predictably, behind-the-scenes stills from these films were as close to candid as their publicists would allow. It was possible to see that Judy Garland was excited to be in Oz, that Clark Gable did not like director George Cukor (the jovial man who can be seen on page 84 directing Vivien Leigh and Gable from the camera dolly), and that Selznick was driving Victor Fleming (Cukor's replacement, who can be seen on page 85 directing Leigh and Gable) to a nervous breakdown. The Hollywood camera, so adept at dissembling, was not lying this time, but it was selling tickets.

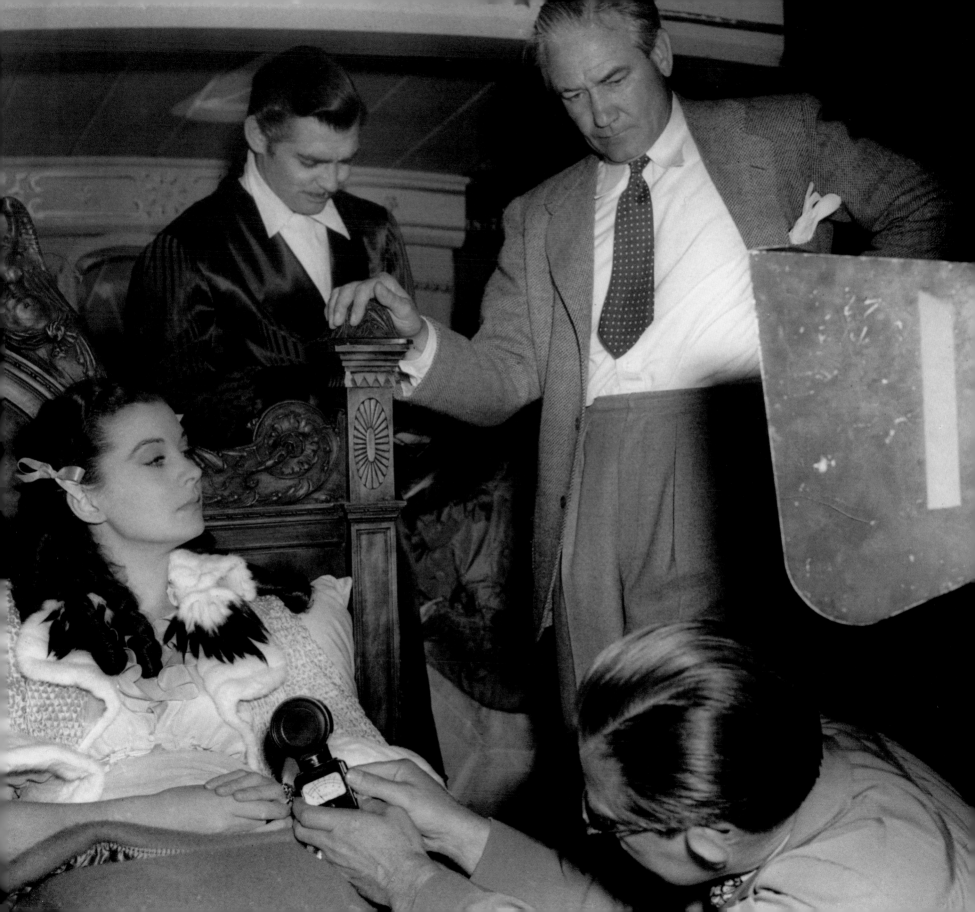

EACH DAWN I DIE | 19**39** | WARNER BROS.

Director William Keighley (with cane) gives last-minute instructions on the set to James Cagney, who plays a journalist wrongly jailed. Whatever scintillation the story lacked, Cagney made up for it with his usual powerful delivery. In all, Cagney and Keighley made six films together for Warner Bros.

EACH DAWN I DIE | 1939 | WARNER BROS.

William Keighley with cons James Cagney and George Raft moments before starting a scene

THE HUNCHBACK OF NOTRE DAME | 1939 | RKO

William Dieterle had a formidable task not only adapting Victor Hugo's oft-read tale, but in
forging a version that would be every bit as noble as the silent of 1923, starring Lon Chaney
as Quasimodo. Dieterle succeeded. Medieval France was lavishly re-created, as seen here in
this tracking shot. Charles Laughton played the kindhearted Quasimodo, and Maureen O'Hara,
in her American film debut, convincingly portrayed the gypsy Esmeralda.

THE LETTER | 19**40** | WARNER BROS.

After their successful collaboration on *Jezebel*, director William Wyler and Bette Davis tackled a steamy tropical story by W. Somerset Maugham, *The Letter*. Few directors knew better than Wyler where to place a camera for maximum dramatic effect. In this scene he conveys the tension in an airless courtroom as a murder trial verdict is announced. Note how the still photographer also directs our eyes to Davis (in hat) by angling the heads and eyes of her coworkers toward her.

CITIZEN KANE 19**41** RKO

With *Citizen Kane*, Orson Welles set a new standard in filmmaking and in so doing made
what many consider the finest, most influential American movie. The accomplishments of the film
are profound, from the innovative approach to unveiling Kane's story, to the technical advances
in lighting and camera work. At this moment, Welles—who was only twenty-four when he began
working on the picture—looks down from a camera crane at a mass of old newspapers,
intended as part of a montage sequence.

CITIZEN KANE | 19**41** | RKO

The one-man band Orson Welles (he cowrote, produced, directed, and starred in *Kane*)
on the set with his favorite cinematographer, Gregg Toland, whose innovative camera made
possible the dramatic long shots in the movie.

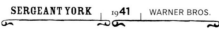

SERGEANT YORK | 19**41** | WARNER BROS.

The real Sergeant Alvin York was one of the most decorated World War I heroes, and when
he sold Warner Bros. the rights to his story, he insisted among other things that his character be
played by Gary Cooper. It was, and with such humanity that Cooper later received an Academy
Award for Best Actor. Director Howard Hawks, seated here on a platform, is directing a scene with
Cooper. *Sergeant York* was nominated for eleven Academy Awards.

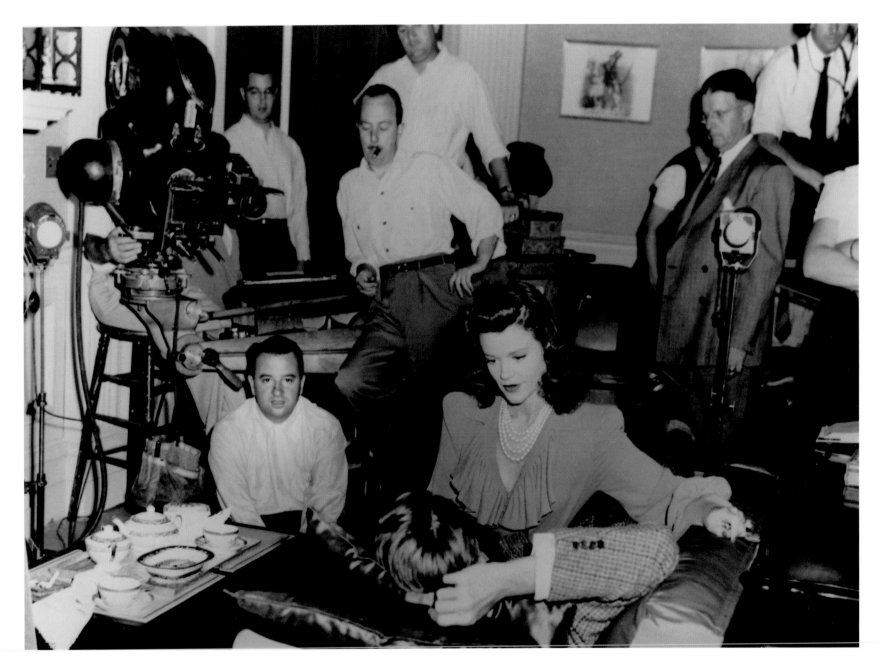

CAT PEOPLE | 19**42** | RKO

Simone Simon played the bewitching Cat Woman in producer Val Lewton's crime suspense film.
A hallmark of a Lewton film was its use of suggestion, shadow, and atmosphere rather than
outright horror. Jacques Tourneur (looking at the still photographer) went on to direct two
more films for Lewton: *I Walked with a Zombie* and *The Leopard Man.*

as a mixed blessing to Hollywood. The film capital lost a
g men but gained an audience flush with war plant dollars.
londe and *Meet Me in St. Louis*, lighthearted films set in an
re escapist fare for a nation worrying about its men in
e war effort mandated propaganda. Warner Bros., long
opical films, made war films like *Across the Pacific*, which
the Humphrey Bogart phenomenon of *The Maltese Falcon*
in the pan. Shortly after Pearl Harbor, producer Hal
ome interested in an obscure play called *Everybody Comes to*
of a disillusioned American expatriate who revisits his
s the Nazis. In 1942, Wallis decided to tailor the story to
guy persona. Envisioning the project as "a romantic story
ing," Wallis renamed it *Casablanca*.

hy still photographer at Warner Bros. could attest, Bogart's
not assumed for the camera. Twelve frustrating years in
n underpaid and unappreciated supporting player had
r and sarcastic. "In my first thirty-four pictures," he said,
twelve, electrocuted or hanged in eight, and was a jailbird
he Little Lord Fauntleroy of the Lot." With the encour-
w drinks, he would become contentious, especially if his
bed and alcoholic Mayo Methot, was needling him.

On *Casablanca*, the job of the still photo
stills that showed an efficient, harmonious product
best efforts, this film was anything but. It was beh
over an uncompleted script, and plagued by quarre
constantly about the dialogue," wrote Wallis years
saying that they had no idea what they were doing
Bogart was David O. Selznick's Swedish discovery,
who sometimes achieved a dreamy performance by
her leading man. On this film she was too confuse
too anxious to get the starring role in *For Whom the*
Gary Cooper) to be more than cordial to Bogart.
unresolved ending, she did not know if she would
arms or those of Paul Henreid, who was playing a

Casablanca's behind-the-scenes stills rever
mid-1930s—posed, formal, glamorous. In this wa
disguised the tension on the set that often escalate
between Bogart and director Michael Curtiz. Wall
arguments, expecting that Curtiz would deliver as l
The Adventures of Robin Hood. Everyone was taken by
a few weeks before the film's premiere, invaded the
made the film's title synonymous with victory; *Cas*

Foll

C. Pub 2

DESPERATE JOURNEY | 19**42** | WARNER BROS.

Actor Raymond Massey (at desk) rehearses an interrogation scene with wartime
prisoners performed by Alan Hale Sr., Arthur Kennedy, Errol Flynn, Ronald Reagan,
and Ronald Sinclair.

YANKEE DOODLE DANDY | 19**42** | WARNER BROS.

Jeanne Cagney, James Cagney, Joan Leslie, Walter Huston (as Uncle Sam), and
Rosemary DeCamp (as Lady Liberty) prepare for the finale song, "You're a Grand Old Flag."
The biopic also included such enduring songs as "Give My Regards to Broadway" and the
title song, "Yankee Doodle Dandy." Cagney's sister, Jeanne, played his on-screen sister, and
his brother, William, was the film's associate producer.

NOW, VOYAGER | 19**42** | WARNER BROS.

Director Irving Rapper (seated) chats with Paul Henreid and Bette Davis on the deck of the ship set.
By this time in her career, Davis was accustomed to fighting for the parts she wanted (she'd previously
been engaged in a notorious battle with Warner Bros. on the subject) and she very much wanted
to play Charlotte in this film version of Olive Higgins Prouty's novel when she read that Irene Dunne
was being considered. Davis got the part and later the Oscar nomination for Best Actress.
She had already received Academy Awards for her work in *Dangerous* and *Jezebel*.

WOMAN OF THE YEAR | 19**42** | MGM

The first of their nine pairings on screen, this Katharine Hepburn–Spencer Tracy vehicle is
widely considered one of their best. Sparks fly and cultures clash when a worldly and sophisticated
political columnist (Hepburn) challenges the opinions of a low-key but impassioned sportswriter
(Tracy). Romance, comedy, and compromise ensue as they attempt to make a life together.
Directed by George Stevens (seen with a pipe).

KEEPER OF THE FLAME | 19**42** | MGM

Director George Cukor gives child actor Darryl Hickman direction, while Spencer Tracy provides
off-camera support in this mystery surrounding the life and death of a well-known war patriot.

WHISTLING IN DIXIE | 19**42** | MGM

Comedian Red Skelton became a movie star with the MGM "Whistling" series, of which
Whistling in Dixie was the second. Here, Ann Rutherford, George Bancroft, Skelton, "Rags" Ragland,
and Diana Lewis prepare to be submerged in water in a mock cellar.

FOR ME AND MY GAL | 19**42** | MGM

In this Busby Berkeley musical, a young Gene Kelly does his first on-screen hoofing and Judy Garland
proves that she has unquestionably moved from juvenile to adult roles. Before she worked on this
World War I period musical, Garland had entertained World War II troops stationed in the Midwest.

GIRL CRAZY | 19**43** | MGM

Judy Garland and Mickey Rooney on either side of Tommy Dorsey while rehearsing the
"I Got Rhythm" number. Norman Taurog directed, but the military style of choreographer
Busby Berkeley is evident. The camera riding the crane glides over the performers.

CABIN IN THE SKY | 1943 | MGM

Cabin in the Sky is notable for being an all-black musical and for the debut of Vincente Minnelli,
a young up-and-coming director who had previously worked on Broadway. Minnelli's talent
for composition, his eye for production values, and his attention to detail helped shape the film
into a success in its day. The movie was also a showcase for tremendous talents Ethel Waters
and Lena Horne and includes a cameo by Louis Armstrong. Waters awaits direction on stage
with Eddie "Rochester" Anderson.

THOUSANDS CHEER | 19**43** | MGM

As Eddie Marsh, Gene Kelly stages a musical for his fellow servicemen. MGM heavyweights
appear throughout the film, some as characters and others as themselves. Lena Horne, as herself,
is lip-synching the mesmerizing "Honeysuckle Rose" for director George Sidney. To the right of
Sidney is the script girl, who is watching to make sure that Horne's gestures match from take to take.
Other luminaries in the film: Mickey Rooney, Lucille Ball, Judy Garland, Red Skelton, Ann Sothern,
June Allyson, Bob Crosby and His Bobcats, and Kay Kyser and His Orchestra.

NATIONAL VELVET ~ 19**44** | MGM

Elizabeth Taylor stands with King Charles, the horse she rode to glory in this heartwarming film.
Standing behind her on location at Pebble Beach, California, is director Clarence Brown. Seated to
his left is the script girl, and, to his right, Mickey Rooney leans on a stool. Taylor, who has had a lifelong
love of animals, persuaded MGM to give her this horse as a birthday gift when filming ended.
She was born in England, where she had left behind a horse when her family moved to Beverly Hills.
Her first film at MGM, *Lassie Come Home,* was based on an animal story by another Brit, Eric Knight.

GASLIGHT | 19**44** | MGM

A posed production still, rare by this time, shows George Cukor directing Ingrid Bergman and Charles Boyer from the top of the stairs. This romantic honeymoon scene, beautifully lit by cinematographer Joseph Ruttenberg (sitting next to camera), gives no hint of the drama to come. Bergman won an Academy Award for her performance as a woman slowly being driven insane by a conniving husband. MGM made this film only four years after a well-received British version of *Gaslight* starring Diana Wynyard and Anton Walbrook. The studio minimized its risks by buying the rights to, and all existing prints of, the 1940 film.

110

THIRTY SECONDS OVER TOKYO | 19**44** | MGM

Gordon McDonald and Don DeFore wait for a take in a mock-up of the *Ruptured Duck,* the bomber
that was commanded by Van Johnson as Captain Ted W. Lawson in this World War II movie about
the first American attack on Japan. Spencer Tracy makes a guest appearance as General Doolittle.
Thirty Seconds won an Academy Award for Best Visual Effects.

THEY WERE EXPENDABLE | 19**45** | MGM

When William White's book *They Were Expendable* was published in 1942, director John Ford was serving in the
Field Photographic Branch of the Office of Strategic Services during World War II and directing the famous
war documentaries *December 7th* and *The Battle of Midway*, both Oscar winners. In *They Were Expendable* his credit
appears as "Directed by John Ford, Captain U.S.N.R." Several other names in the credits also appear with their
military ranks, and the entire production has a feel of great authenticity. Ford shot much of this feature in
Key Biscayne, Florida, and when he broke his shin, actor Robert Montgomery assumed directorial chores.

THE PICTURE OF DORIAN GRAY | 19**45** | MGM

Director Albert Lewin faced an uphill battle in filming Oscar Wilde's sexually ambiguous
morality tale at Louis B. Mayer's MGM, the home of homespun virtue. Surprisingly, Mayer gave
Lewin carte blanche to bring Wilde's hothouse flowers to life. After being turned down by
Montgomery Clift, Lewin cast the unknown Hurd Hatfield (here with Angela Lansbury) in the
most expensive horror film of Hollywood's Golden Era. The lavishly mounted, unnerving film
was a huge hit and became one of Mayer's favorites.

SARATOGA TRUNK | 19**45** | MGM

Ingrid Bergman costars with Gary Cooper as director Sam Wood and cinematographer
Ernest Haller (in glasses) watch. Though the film was made in 1943, it was not released until
1945 owing to a backlog of movies made during World War II. It was, however, shown to
servicemen overseas during the two-year hiatus.

114

WEEK-END AT THE WALDORF | 19**45** | MGM

Echoes of the star teaming and hotel setting created by *Grand Hotel* (1932) were evident in this
film, and the formula still worked. Lana Turner (Joan Crawford's Flaemmchen in *Grand Hotel*) and
Van Johnson rehearse a scene on the Starlight Roof set as director Robert Z. Leonard watches
(in dark jacket). The script girl has her back to the camera. Note the use of a "baby spot" above
Johnson's head, which is trained on Turner to create a softer, more attractive look.

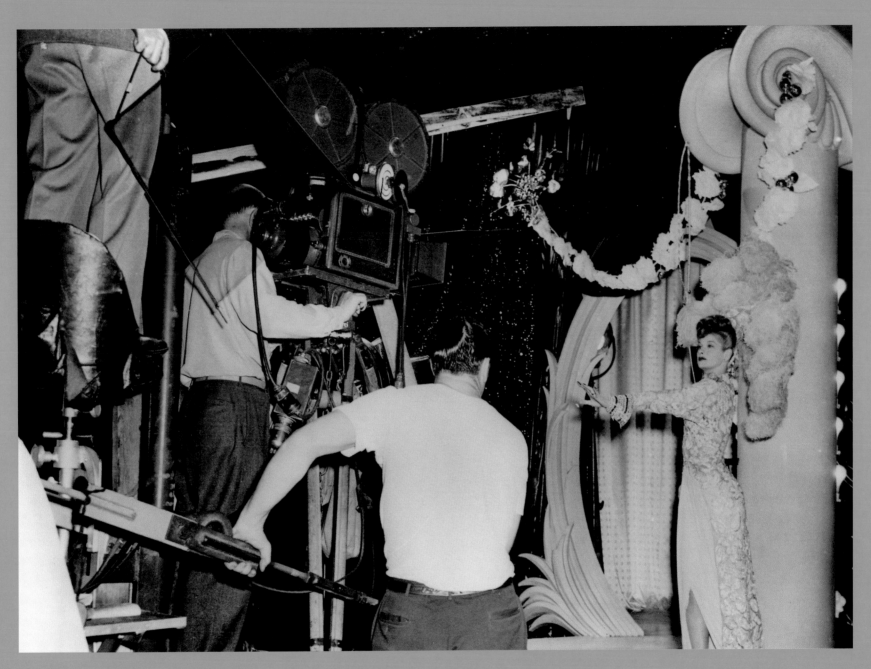

ZIEGFELD FOLLIES 19**46** MGM

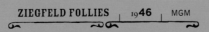

In the years before she came to be known to Americans simply as Lucy, Lucille Ball was a contract
player for MGM. Much in the same vein as *The Hollywood Revue of 1929*, MGM's *Ziegfeld Follies* was an
all-star showcase, with William Powell playing impresario Flo Ziegfeld. The mix of stars included
Ball, shown here rehearsing the production number "Here's to the Girls."

ZIEGFELD FOLLIES | 19**46** | MGM

Gene Kelly and Fred Astaire rehearse "The Babbitt and the Bromide"
for cinematographer George Folsey and director Vincente Minnelli.

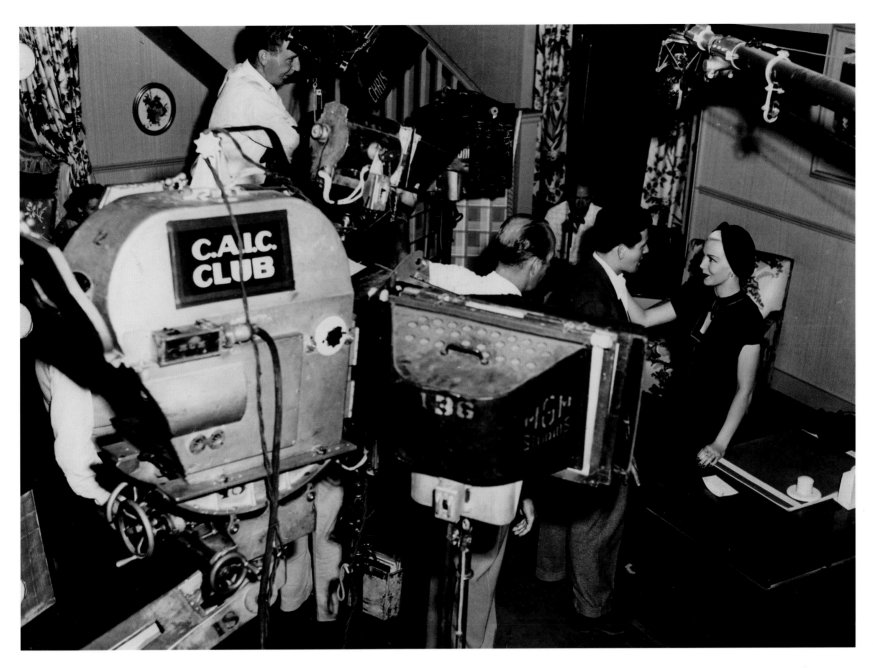

THE POSTMAN ALWAYS RINGS TWICE | 19**46** | MGM

Although MGM secured the rights to pulp novelist James M. Cain's hard-bitten murder romance
The Postman Always Rings Twice in 1934, it wasn't until twelve years later that the film finally made it to the
screen. A notoriously nasty story, rife with sexual intrigue, *Postman* involves drifter Frank Chambers (John
Garfield), who conspires with femme fatale Cora Smith (Lana Turner) to murder her husband. Director Tay
Garnett's steamy film noir with its explicit sexuality just made it past the censors, thanks to Turner being
shown wearing white. In this rare still, the actress is in black, a reflection of her dark character.

LADY IN THE LAKE | 19**46** | MGM

Actor Robert Montgomery, in his directorial debut, played Raymond Chandler's famous gumshoe, private detective Philip Marlowe. *Lady in the Lake* is exceptional for Montgomery's use of subjective camera throughout the entire film. In effect, whatever Marlowe saw or experienced, so did the audience. Marlowe's voice was heard in his voice-over narratives, and he was only seen when reflected in mirrors. Here, actor Lloyd Nolan as tough cop Lieutenant DeGarmot takes aim at Marlowe.

OUT OF THE PAST | 19**47** | RKO

An innocent beach scene at Sequit Point, California, was one of the few upbeat moments for
Robert Mitchum and Jane Greer (back to camera) in Daniel Mainwaring's detective story
Build My Gallows High. It reached the screen as *Out of the Past,* and with Kirk Douglas completing
the triangle, this masterly film directed by Jacques Tourneur had all the elements of a hit but was
given the cold shoulder by postwar audiences, who still preferred escapist fare to poetic evocations
of evil. Not until the 1970s was it acclaimed as a masterpiece of film noir.

Casablanca brought Humphrey Bogart to stardom. What kept him there were roles like the one he had played in *The Maltese Falcon*—a cynical idealist maneuvering his way through a corrupt, seductive city. He was finally in the right place at the right time. Audiences were ready for something stronger than the breezy *Thin Man* series, and studios turned from elegant *Thin Man* author Dashiell Hammett to mordant Raymond Chandler *(Lady in the Lake)* and sardonic James M. Cain *(The Postman Always Rings Twice)*. Their films were called detective dramas—the term "film noir" was decades away—but their grubby gumshoes were a far cry from the glossy optimism of *The Thin Man's* William Powell. In films like *Murder, My Sweet* and *Out of the Past,* Dick Powell and Robert Mitchum grappled not only with the evil in an oily adversary, but also with the venality and lust in themselves. What aroused that lust were the black-widow charms of slinky enigmas like Claire Trevor and Jane Greer, amoral dolls who lived only to cross and double-cross.

Beginning with 1945's *To Have and Have Not,* Bogart and his sexy nineteen-year-old costar Lauren Bacall changed this formula. Bacall was not a femme fatale and Bogart, while attracted to her, was not a fatalistic moth zooming toward a sultry flame. This unlikely couple was having fun, both courting and crime fighting. Still photographers like Bert Longworth also had fun chronicling the progress of an on-screen chemistry that soon sparked a real-life romance. By the time of 1947's *Dark Passage* Bogart and Bacall were married.

Dark Passage was shot on location in San Francisco by director Delmer Daves, who chose to begin the film with a subjective camera; the audience would see through Bogart's eyes as he escaped San Quentin and endured plastic surgery in order to track down his wife's killer and clear himself. "I can just hear Jack Warner scream," Bogart said when he read the script. "He's paying me all this money to make the picture and nobody will even see me until it's a third over." Having earned $467,361 in 1946, Bogart was the world's highest-paid actor, so the unit still photographer made sure that the public saw a lot of him, even though Warner had recently told the publicity department to shoot and print fewer stills. There was another consideration. Bogart had recently been diagnosed with alopecia, so it was important that his new hairpiece look natural. "I never appear professionally without it because that guy up there on the screen has a full head of hair," he said, referring to the image he had worked so long to create.

122

CROSSFIRE | 19**47** | RKO

Edward Dmytryk's look at anti-Semitism in the military had all the trappings of what would later be
called film noir: intrigue, murder, and a sexy leading lady. Gloria Grahame, seen here with George Cooper,
received an Academy Award nomination for her performance as a confused "B-girl" (the 1940s expression
"bar girl" was used since the Production Code frowned on the depiction of prostitutes). This production
still shows how close the big Mitchell camera would sometimes come to actors in order to capture a detail,
in this case on the table. Close-ups, however, were shot with a long lens and from a respectful distance.

THEY WON'T BELIEVE ME | 19**47** | RKO

Robert Young and Rita Johnson prepare to shoot a scene in a car. In the filmed sequence,
a station wagon was substituted. Fans of *Father Knows Best* or *Marcus Welby, M.D.*, would have to go
back twenty years in Young's career to find him starring in this role as a cad, a husband whose
cheating leads to a betrayal of three women, including Johnson, who plays his wife.

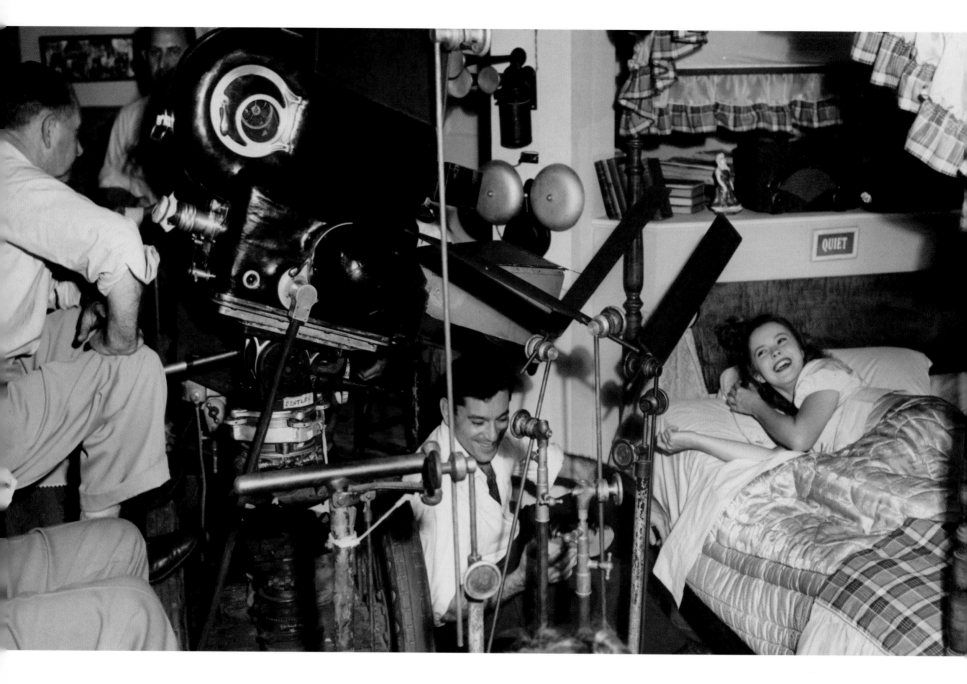

THE BACHELOR AND THE BOBBY-SOXER | 19**47** | RKO

By casting Shirley Temple as a bobby-soxer opposite Cary Grant, RKO hoped to capture a
teenage audience and recapture a world of Temple fans. The awesomely talented tot had won
these fans thirteen years earlier when her dimples, blonde curls, and refreshing honesty graced
such hits as *Baby Take a Bow*—and saved foundering Fox Film. She continued to be a box-office
bonanza when the company became Twentieth Century-Fox, but production head
Darryl F. Zanuck let her go when she reached "that awkward age."

KEY LARGO | 19**48** | WARNER BROS.

Humphrey Bogart was the romantic antiromantic who provided the moral center of so many films of the 1940s. This was no less so in *Key Largo*, in which he starred with Lauren Bacall, Lionel Barrymore, Edward G. Robinson, and Claire Trevor. Here, he is seen with Bacall and Barrymore (draped in a blanket), and director John Huston. Bogart and Huston worked together on six films, of which *Key Largo* was the fourth. Cinematographer Karl Freund stands to Huston's right.

KEY LARGO | 19**48** | WARNER BROS.

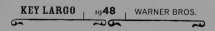

Humphrey Bogart and Lauren Bacall with Felipa Gomez wait to start a scene. Movie audiences were
treated to four films starring the offscreen couple, *Key Largo* being the last. The ramshackle hotel
where most of the film's drama unfolds was constructed on the Warner Bros. lot along with the beach
area seen in this still. Exterior shots of the hurricane sequences were actually taken from stock
footage used in *Night Unto Night*, a Ronald Reagan melodrama made the same year at Warner Bros.

MR. BLANDINGS BUILDS HIS DREAM HOUSE | 19**48** | RKO

Cary Grant, Myrna Loy, and Sharyn Moffett (as Jim, Muriel, and Joan Blandings)
wait in a car for the scene to begin. The script girl hovers nearby (in flowered skirt).
This was the last of three movies that Loy and Grant appeared in together.

Few individuals in Hollywood history have had as much influence on the musical film as producer Arthur Freed or Gene Kelly. Freed had come to MGM with the early talkies, when he and Nacio Herb Brown coauthored such standards as "Singin' in the Rain." The success of Freed's 1939 production, *Babes in Arms* with Judy Garland and Mickey Rooney, elevated him to his own production unit. He soon enlisted the services of Kelly, the choreographer and star of Broadway's *Pal Joey.* Under Freed's guidance, Kelly became a movie star who could act, dance, and direct.

The team had hit after hit—*For Me and My Gal, Anchors Aweigh, The Pirate*—but by 1949 television was making threatening inroads into the movies' domain. Hollywood needed to recapture its straying audience by offering something that could not be seen on TV. Freed and Kelly looked for a property that would dazzle America. MGM owned the Betty Comden–Adolph Green–Leonard Bernstein play *On the Town,* the happy story of three sailors on leave in New York City. The studio with twenty-eight soundstages and two back lots planned to create a Manhattan right in Culver City. Kelly and codirector Stanley Donen had other plans; Freed made them happen.

"This film was a milestone," recalled Kelly in 1977, "the first musical to be shot on location. We took the musical off the soundstage and showed that it could be realistic. . . . We showed sailors getting off the ship in the Brooklyn Navy Yard and singing and dancing through the streets of New York. You can't imagine how crazy everybody thought this was at the time." *On the Town* was shot in Technicolor, which meant that the elephantine three-strip camera had to be choreographed as carefully as the dancers. Temperature, humidity, and angles of sunlight all had to be plotted on the sidewalks of New York. "There was no stage, no theater, simply the street," recalled Donen.

Capturing all this action with a 4x5 press camera was the unit still photographer, who made certain that his behind-the-scenes photos prominently featured landmarks such as the Statue of Liberty, the Bronx Zoo, and Rockefeller Center (pictured), where crowds of fans leaned over railings to see singing idol Frank Sinatra. For him and his costars, performing in public was a rare pleasure. They enjoyed the enthusiastic audience that actors rarely have on a quiet soundstage. One scene was shot at Radio City, where the film opened months later to a record-breaking crowd of ten thousand people, many of whom had watched *On the Town* being shot.

NEPTUNE'S DAUGHTER | 19**49** | MGM

Esther Williams perfected the musical mermaid image in the great MGM swimming movies of
the 1940s and 1950s. This former member of the Los Angeles Aquacade made a soft film debut
in one of the Andy Hardy films in 1942 and came into her own in *Bathing Beauty,* two years later.
In this scene from *Neptune's Daughter,* the swimmers run through the final sequence in which they will
be joined by Williams (at bottom, center; behind couple at table) and Ricardo Montalban.

SUMMER STOCK | 19**50** | MGM

Judy Garland was notorious for her weight fluctuations, and for *Summer Stock* she lost more than fifteen pounds before filming the famous production number "Get Happy." The scene was shot a few weeks after the rest of the production on the film had wrapped. It was also the last number that Garland would shoot at MGM after fourteen years under contract to the studio.

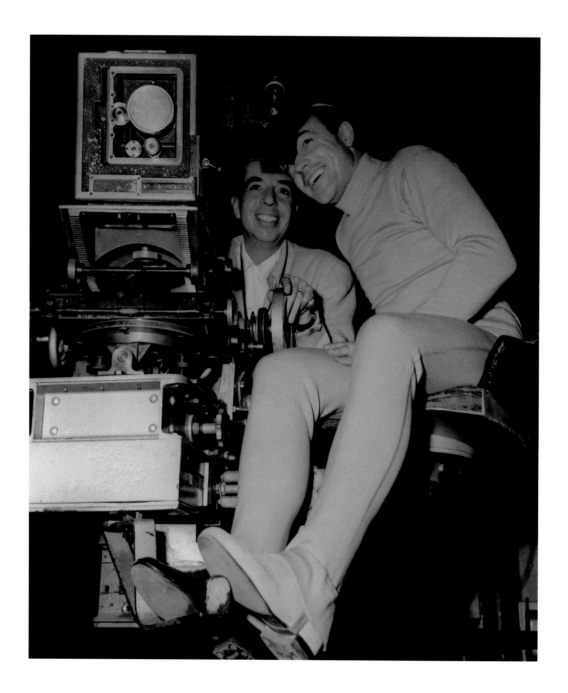

AN AMERICAN IN PARIS | 19**51** | MGM

Gene Kelly peers through the viewfinder of the massive three-strip Technicolor camera. Behind him is
director Vincente Minnelli, with whom he worked on this tribute to the late George Gershwin. The scene
they are filming is the spectacular seventeen-minute ballet sequence, a tour de force of choreography,
lighting, color, and camera movement. The supreme achievement of the Arthur Freed musical unit at
MGM, *An American in Paris* was a collaborative work of art that won Academy Awards for Original Story
and Screenplay, Scoring, Costume Design, Art Direction, Color Cinematography, and Best Picture.

HIS KIND OF WOMAN | 19**51** | RKO

Jane Russell and Robert Mitchum costarred in two movies together—*His Kind of Woman* and
Macao, a year later. The hotel set, swimming pool, and beach were all built on a soundstage.
During *His Kind of Woman*, a dispute occurred between coproducer Howard Hughes and
director John Farrow when Hughes told him to reshoot the film for more exposure of Russell.
Farrow quit, and the film was completed by Richard Fleischer.

QUO VADIS | 19**51** | MGM

Director Mervyn LeRoy brought this MGM period epic in at $7 million after shooting in Italy for
six months and using more than five thousand extras. *Quo Vadis* received eight Oscar nominations,
including one for Best Picture. Peter Ustinov, who received a nomination as Best Supporting Actor,
is seen with his back to the camera. Leo Genn, who also received a Best Supporting Actor Oscar
nomination, is to Ustinov's left, Ralph Truman is to his right, and Patricia Laffan reclines on a divan.

CLASH BY NIGHT | 19**52** | RKO

As the star of such films as *Stella Dallas, Meet John Doe,* and *Double Indemnity,* Barbara Stanwyck was
known to audiences for her tough but softhearted demeanor and her gutsy, deep-voiced delivery.
In Fritz Lang's *Clash by Night,* she was no less brilliant, bringing pathos and credibility to the role of
an unhappily married woman. She is shown here on location in Monterey, California.

BAD DAY AT BLACK ROCK | 19**55** | MGM

Good versus evil clashes again on the screen, this time in a John Sturges potboiler, set in the fictional
western town of Black Rock, California. Sturges, director of such powerful films as *The Magnificent
Seven* and *The Great Escape,* received his only Oscar nomination for this film. Spencer Tracy is seen here
with Robert Ryan on location in Lone Pine, California. Sturges is seated, wearing sunglasses. The sun
was so fierce on the set that with lights the temperature reached 125 degrees.

BLACKBOARD JUNGLE | 19**55** | WARNER BROS.

Blackboard Jungle was the first major Hollywood picture to portray the problems of inner-city schools and, along with the film *Rebel Without a Cause* (1955), depicted with gritty reality the disenfranchised teens of the 1950s. Seen here are Glenn Ford, who plays a high school teacher determined to restore order in his classroom, and Anne Francis as his pregnant wife. The film is notable for being one of the first to use rock 'n' roll in the soundtrack—"Rock Around the Clock" by Bill Haley and the Comets accompanied the opening credits, paving the way for the song's popularity.

REBEL WITHOUT A CAUSE | 19**55** | WARNER BROS.

Nicholas Ray masterfully directed James Dean and Natalie Wood in one of the cinema's most
enduring troubled-youth pictures, *Rebel Without a Cause*. The film launched James Dean's career even
while signaling its abrupt end. Released just one month after Dean died in a car accident near
Paso Robles, California, at the age of twenty-four, the film captured the young star's astounding
screen magnetism and tinderbox emotions, as well as the angst of an entire generation.

LOVE ME OR LEAVE ME | 19**55** | WARNER BROS.

Doris Day played against type in this stinging true-life story of Ruth Etting, a blues singer in the
1920s and 1930s, and her cruel gangster husband, Martin Snyder (James Cagney). Day, who in fact was
discovered by Michael Curtiz while she was singing, had made a name for herself acting in Warner Bros.
musicals. But she wanted to work with Cagney (the two had previously appeared together in *The West
Point Story*, 1950), which resulted in this more serious and complex role for her. In this image, Cagney
and Day speak with director Charles Vidor as they prepare to shoot Day's visit to Cagney in prison.

IT'S ALWAYS FAIR WEATHER | 19**55** | MGM

Gene Kelly and Stanley Donen shared credit for directing this Betty Comden and Adolph Green musical. Both men are seen here watching Dolores Gray rehearse a scene with Michael Kidd, Cyd Charisse, and Dan Dailey. Memorable songs "Thanks a Lot But No Thanks" (Gray) and "Baby, You Knock Me Out" (Charisse) and the famous ash-can sequence do much to enliven the story.

THE SEARCHERS | 19**56** | WARNER BROS.

The unit still photographer on any John Ford film had the responsibility of capturing both
his stars and the awesome terrain to which the director brought his repertory company.
Here, in Monument Valley, Ford shows how he wants Vera Miles to embrace Jeffrey Hunter
while Olive Carey looks on. *The Searchers* was filmed in color, but the eloquence of Ford's imagery
translated equally well to black-and-white publicity stills.

By the mid-1950s the Hollywood photo was still an 8x10 glossy, but it no longer originated in an 8x10 camera. Most movie stills were now shot with Rolleiflex 2¼x2¼ cameras. The easy-to-load roll film was now the standard for behind-the-scenes photos. Approved shots were printed to 8x10 size, and an 8x10 copy negative was then made of each so that the studio contact printer could hit its thousand-print quota. The unit still photographer also had to field an invasion of photojournalists. Magazines like the *Saturday Evening Post* insisted on sending their own employees to Hollywood, saying that stills supplied by the studios were not spontaneous enough. What they meant was that they were not honest enough. With the increased emphasis on movie-star scandals brought about by tabloids like *Hollywood Confidential*, editors wanted photos that exposed what studio publicists were trying to hide: namely that movie people were spoiled, irresponsible, out-of-control children. There were plenty of them on the set of the Warner Bros. film *Giant*.

Edna Ferber's multigenerational Texas novel of cattle, oil, and racism promised to become the Hollywood epic of the fifties, with director George Stevens crafting a saga worthy of its title. Its three stars were blazing with celebrity. Rock Hudson was fresh from *Magnificent Obsession;* James Dean fresh from *East of Eden;* and Elizabeth Taylor still fresh after twelve years at MGM, two husbands, and numerous broken hearts, all of which she explained away by saying: "I have a woman's body and a child's emotions."

Stevens made a point of favoring the inexperienced Hudson, who had to carry the film, but he spared no one the tedious, rigorous direction that was his trademark. Hudson, who had to age thirty years on-screen, was grateful for the attention after five years of hack directors but later quipped: "Working with Stevens is an aging process in itself." Dean, a Method actor, immediately clashed with Stevens over his approach to the role. Stevens left Dean sitting for a whole day "like a bump on a log watching that big lumpy Rock Hudson make love to Liz Taylor." Taylor had met Hudson's fiancée but sensed that the marriage was being arranged by his manager to avert an exposé of his homosexuality in *Hollywood Confidential*. Photographers wanting a shot of the equally ambiguous Dean had to beg him to remove his glasses; he rarely cooperated. On location in Texas, Dean became friends with Taylor but could not wait to finish his scenes and return to California to participate in an auto race. He died, aged twenty-four, in an accident en route. The cast of *Giant* received the news in a projection room. Stevens responded: "He had it coming to him. The way he drove, he had it coming." The director further shocked Taylor by requiring her to work the next day. Taylor got through her scene, then screamed at him: "I hope you rot in hell!" Despite publicists' pruning, *Giant's* stills did reveal the turmoil behind the scenes.

Ironically, "high society" is exactly what Grace Kelly was launched into following completion of this
Cole Porter musical remake of Philip Barry's *The Philadelphia Story* (1940). *High Society* was Kelly's last film
appearance before becoming Her Serene Highness, Princess of Monaco. At left, the ring seen on Ms. Kelly's
hand was her actual engagement ring from fiancé Prince Rainier. At right, Frank Sinatra and Grace Kelly
prepare for a scene with director Charles Walters. This film also marked the first time the world's two most
famous pop singers, Bing Crosby (in still, left) and Frank Sinatra (in still, right), appeared and sang together.

GIGI | 19**58** | MGM

To bring Colette's whimsical tale of innocence and worldliness to the screen, Vincente Minnelli had to re-create the Paris of La Belle Époque—in Paris. It took MGM's vast resources and the talents of veterans such as Louis Jourdan, Maurice Chevalier (seated on carriage), and cinematographer Joseph Ruttenberg (seated above them) to make the last of the great MGM musicals. Leslie Caron's Gigi and Minnelli's make-believe world entranced a real world of moviegoers, earning nine Academy Awards

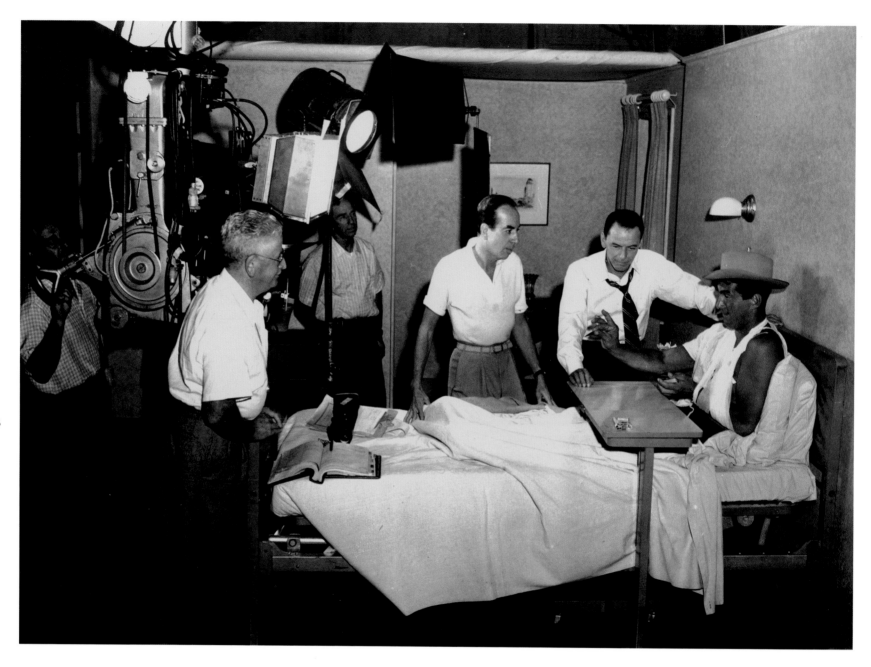

SOME CAME RUNNING | 19**58** | MGM

Some Came Running, a serious postwar film, was a departure from musicals for director
Vincente Minnelli. It was also the first of ten films Frank Sinatra made with Dean Martin and the
second of ten with cinematographer William Daniels, shown here standing at the foot of the bed.

NORTH BY NORTHWEST | 19**59** | MGM

Alfred Hitchcock felt that *Vertigo* had failed because James Stewart was too old for the part.
With Cary Grant, his favorite, back in harness, the Master of Suspense wove another variation
on his well-known theme, a man unexpectedly and undeservedly caught in a sticky web of
intrigue. Avoiding the clichés of dark alleys, *North by Northwest* challenged its hapless hero,
Roger O. Thornhill, in bright, sunny, colorful settings while Hitchcock's meticulous storyboards
brought order to the chaos of a crowded movie set.

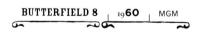

BUTTERFIELD 8 | 19**60** | MGM

Butterfield 8 was the film Elizabeth Taylor did not want to do. She was still grieving the loss of her husband, producer Mike Todd, in a private-plane crash, and she considered the John O'Hara novel beneath her, but producer Pandro Berman prevailed on her to make the film. Nonetheless, she turned in an Oscar-winning performance. Taylor is seen in this behind-the-scenes shot with costar Laurence Harvey on location in New York.

HOW THE WEST WAS WON | 19**62** | MGM

How the West Was Won was an all-star epic directed by three veterans of the genre: John Ford, George Marshall, and Henry Hathaway. Ford, seen here talking to actress Carroll Baker, directed the Civil War segments of the movie in just fourteen days. George Peppard (here with a dog) played Baker's son, though at thirty-three, he was more than two years older than she. The film was shot in Cinerama, a wide-screen process that used three cameras with interlocked shutters and had to be exhibited with three separate projectors.

In the 1960s Hollywood was no longer an empire of moguls. It was a jungle of superagents, cutthroat deals, and corporate buyouts. To these upstarts, cutting costs was more important than glamour, and publicity photos, long considered a luxury, were the first to feel the knife. Unit still photographers were now permitted to use only 35mm cameras. These small-format negatives yielded prints that were grainy and fuzzy; no one cared.

One exception was the MGM superproduction *Doctor Zhivago*, which allowed the use of medium-format Hasselblad cameras. Part of the credit was due studio president Robert O'Brien, who gave director David Lean free rein after viewing the film's first scenes: "You only need three great shots in a movie to get an Oscar and you've got them already." Lean's unerring visual sense had earlier won him awards for *Great Expectations* and *Lawrence of Arabia*. As important as an Oscar was to MGM, what it really needed was a hit. The studio was in the same situation as it had been with *Ben-Hur* forty years earlier. Owing to a change in management and a series of flops, it wanted an epic to balance its books.

Doctor Zhivago was a $17 million, 232-day production shot in Spain and Finland. Lean and cinematographer Freddie Young filmed it in Metrocolor. Lean had not wanted color, but increased sales of movies to color television were ending the era of black-and-white. Color stills, however, had been a mainstay of publicity since the 1940s, when the rotogravure section of every major magazine was replaced by a full-color

spread. Generally, the unit still photographer shot only a third of his work in color. *Doctor Zhivago* used color stills extensively, gaining coveted space in *Life* and *Look*.

Lean used color to express the emotions of his Russian poet hero (Omar Sharif), his wife (Geraldine Chaplin), and his lover (Julie Christie). One memorable scene took place in a cottage that had been frozen both inside and out, an "ice palace" made inhabitable by Sharif and Christie's passion for each other. Young wanted the interiors to glow with warmth, but Lean insisted that only the multihued coming of spring should bring color to them. "We went in there and sprayed everything gray—took out all the colors," said Lean. The finished scene was one of the most moving in the film, which became the $200 million hit that MGM had hoped for.

Credit for its success was surely due to the widespread dissemination of still photographs. One had to hide in a cellar not to see the delicately etched images of Christie and Chaplin appearing everywhere. Particularly effective was a specially posed and lit shot of Christie and Rod Steiger playing an intimate dinner scene in front of a corps of film artisans. This, and a poignant shot of Christie alighting from a streetcar in the film's final scene, were executed with the same finesse that had characterized the painterly view camera work of silent-film days. As the studio era drew to a close, the triumph of *Doctor Zhivago* was a tribute to the persuasiveness of the artists who made behind-the-scenes stills into personal works of art.

GIRL HAPPY | 19**65** | MGM

Elvis Presley had been making movies since 1956, with such hits as *Jailhouse Rock* and *Viva Las Vegas*
under his belt. *Girl Happy* was a likable vehicle for the star, seen here with other members of the
film's rock band—Gary Crosby, Jimmy Hawkins, and Joby Baker. Shelley Fabares, on the lounge chair,
made three films with Elvis, beginning with this one. Also in the shot are Mary Ann Mobley and
director Boris Sagal (with cigarette).

WHO'S AFRAID OF VIRGINIA WOOLF? | 19**66** | WARNER BROS.

Mike Nichols made his film directing debut with this project, but he was already a star in his own right as half of the improvisational comedy team Nichols and May. Edward Albee's play, with its unglamorous setting, hateful characters, and adult language, was a gamble for Jack Warner, the last of the studio moguls. The star power of Elizabeth Taylor and Richard Burton made the project go, and when the industry censors would not grant it the required seal of approval, *Who's Afraid of Virginia Woolf?* became the first Hollywood film to play in theaters with an "adults only" policy.

THE DIRTY DOZEN | 19**6**7 | MGM

The sixth-highest-grossing film in the history of MGM was the controversial creation of
maverick director Robert Aldrich, who had apprenticed at the studio twenty-five years earlier.
Now, after working on the fringes of the industry, Aldrich made use of the powerful company's
muscle to tell a story so violent and uncompromising that it was almost rejected by industry censors.
Aldrich's vision arrived at the screen intact in part because he knew how to assemble a superb
ensemble cast. Shown here are Lee Marvin and John Cassavetes.

BULLITT 19**68** | WARNER BROS.

Director Peter Yates, behind the camera at right, shouts instructions as Steve McQueen,
playing Detective Frank Bullitt, prepares to get into a cab (note Robert Duvall as
Weissberg the cab driver). The movie was made entirely on location in San Francisco, with
crowds in attendance throughout filming.

BULLITT | 19**68** | WARNER BROS.

Steve McQueen waits beside a Mustang while the crew prepare for the famous car chase sequence. As McQueen and stunt driver Bill Hickman exceeded up to 115 miles an hour in the chase over the hills of San Francisco, more than forty crew members were needed to keep the streets clear during filming. The Bay Bridge is in the distance at right.

THE END

INDEX

ROBERT OSBORNE is the prime-time host of Turner Classic Movies network and a columnist-critic for *The Hollywood Reporter.* He is known as the official biographer of Oscar, and his latest book, the updated *75 Years of the Oscar,* was written at the special request of the Academy of Motion Picture Arts and Sciences.

ALEXA L. FOREMAN is a senior researcher at Turner Classic Movies and is the author of *Women In Motion* and a contributor to *The St. James Women Filmmakers Encyclopedia* and *International Dictionary of Films and Filmmakers.*

RUTH A. PELTASON is the president of Bespoke Books, in New York, specializing in books on the cultural arts. She was previously senior editor and director of Design & Style Books at Harry N. Abrams, Inc., Publishers.

MARK A. VIEIRA is a photographer and film historian specializing in the photographic legacy of Hollywood and author of *Hurrell's Hollywood Portraits, Sin in Soft Focus: Pre-Code Hollywood,* and *Hollywood Horror: From Gothic to Cosmic.*

TURNER CLASSSIC MOVIES is widely considered by film and television critics to be the definitive resource for classic films. Featuring movies from all the major studios (including its own library of Warner Bros., MGM, and RKO) unedited and commercial-free, TCM is available on most cable and satellite systems.
www.turnerclassicmovies.com